IDENTITY AND DIFFERENCE

*This is the fifth publication in the series
"Collected Writings of the Orpheus Institute"
edited by Peter Dejans*

IDENTITY AND DIFFERENCE

Essays on Music,
Language and Time

Jonathan Cross
Jonathan Harvey
Helmut Lachenmann
Albrecht Wellmer
Richard Klein

COLLECTED WRITINGS OF THE
ORPHEUS
INSTITUTE

Leuven University Press
2004

CONTENTS

PREFACE / P. 07

— Jonathan Cross
Writing about Living Composers: Questions, Problems, Contexts / P. 09

— Jonathan Harvey
The Genesis of Quartet No. 4 / P. 43

— Helmut Lachenmann
Philosophy of Composition — Is There Such a Thing? / P. 55

— Albrecht Wellmer
On Music and Language / P. 71

— Richard Klein
Theses on the Relationship Between Music and Time / P. 133

PERSONALIA / P. 189

COLOPHON / P. 192

PREFACE

This volume is a collection of essays based on lectures given at the Orpheus Institute in Ghent at various occasions over the last four years.

Two of our five distinguished authors are British, three are Germans; two are prominent composers, both keen and provocative writers about music; one is a musicologist and daring critic who specializes in contemporary music; two are philosophers and Adorno specialists dealing with such fundamental and highly complex matters as music and language, and music and time.

Quite a mix, you might think, yet I believe it is one with a difference. All authors subscribe to the same seriousness of purpose, and you may find reminiscences of one text in the others, which, I'm sure, will make for a fascinating read. Moreover, this book is all about the current state of music, about thinking, speaking, and writing about music in the immediate aftermath of that stirring and crucial twentieth century.

Allow me to thank my co-editors, Frank Agsteribbe, Sylvester Beelaert and Jeroen D'hoe, the translator, Wieland Hoban, and all those who, in one way or another, contributed to this book.

Peter Dejans

WRITING ABOUT LIVING COMPOSERS: QUESTIONS, PROBLEMS, CONTEXTS

Jonathan Cross

INTRODUCTION

Tracey Emin's unmade bed[1] first came to popular attention when her work was shortlisted for the 1999 Turner Prize, the most prestigious British award in contemporary art. *My Bed* (1998), whose sheets were stained with this controversial artist's own body fluids, was put on display at London's Tate Gallery "surrounded by the detritus of her decadent life,"[2] "the detritus of a life quintessentially her own:"[3] empty vodka bottles, dirty underwear, cigarette packets, condoms and other items of everyday rubbish were scattered around the central mattress.

> ... it was, above all, a confessional. Such links were encouraged by the *mise-en-scène* with its misspelled jottings, declamatory textile and neon, memorabilia, and "home videos" in which the camera wandered, accompanied by voice-overs by the artist, through scenarios of clutter similar to that of *My Bed* and filmed in her apartment near Waterloo station in London, all of which facilitated elisions between life and art and confusions between the two.[4]

The success and/or notoriety of *My Bed* hinged on the authenticity of Tracey's autobiography. Much of the discussion of this particular work in the press (in the UK and the USA) focused on the direct mapping of her life onto her art; but, interestingly, many

---

1. To see a photograph of Tracey Emin's *My Bed*, go to http://www.whitecube.com/html/artists/tre/tre_frset.html
2. John-Paul Stonard, "Tracey Emin", *Grove Dictionary of Art Online* (Oxford University Press, accessed 17 November 2003), http://www.groveart.com
3. Deborah Cherry, "Tracey Emin's *My Bed*, 1998/1999", in: *SHARP* 2 (2002), p. 1; see http://www.sussex.ac.uk/Units/arthist/sharp/issues/0002/pHTML/pTraceyEminMyBed01.shtml (accessed 17 November 2003).
4. ibid.

through its creator. The modern work is consistently presented to us as a mirror of the artist's life.

This behaviour is certainly prevalent in Britain. Though I do not believe it to be a peculiarly British phenomenon, it would seem that our national fascination with biography is rather on the excessive side. Go into any branch of any major bookseller on any British High Street and you will see the biography shelves are extensive; just look at the content of top-selling daily newspapers such as the *Sun* or the *Daily Mail*, or a popular magazine such as *Hello!* The lives of the famous — of so-called "celebrities" — are part of our daily diet. Why should we still be interested in stories about the life and loves of Diana, Princess of Wales, that fill our magazines and TV screens even years after her death? Why does it seem to matter to us so much? Tracey Emin, by presenting her own life story in the shape of her bed, and by transforming it into a work of art, directly confronts us with our own prurient interest in other people's lives. What is the relationship between life and art? To what degree is the biography of the artist embodied in the artwork he or she creates? How should we — the public, the critics — take account of this? *My Bed* asks some very serious and difficult questions of us.

And it also brings into focus important questions for those of us who write about new music. How much — if anything — do we need to know about the life of a living composer? What sort of information should we *expect* to know? How do we interpret that information? How do we assess its appropriateness or validity? Given the fact that it is well-nigh impossible to escape contact with the composer, how does a writer manage that relationship? How, for a musicologist, is it possible to guarantee any kind of scholarly distance? Even if we are prepared to accept that there is some sort of connection between a composer's life and art, how do we know if that composer is telling the "truth", either about his/her life or his/her art?

Before I proceed to examine these questions in more detail, there are some interesting lessons to be learnt from the past. What happens when what a composer says about his own music is taken at face value?

London reviewers also strongly questioned her art's authenticity. One writer discussed her life not only in terms of physical illness and emotional disorder but also as characterised by media celebrity and market success. The art critic Rosemary Betterton, exploring Emin's confessional mode, saw the "autobiographical elements less as direct outpourings and more as highly mediated and artful self-reconstructions."[5]

In trying to understand *My Bed*, we are unable to ignore the story of the living Tracey as she tells it to us. And yet, because this story is mediated through all kinds of art and media institutions, it loses its "authenticity". How, then, can we tell what is "true" or "authentic"? How far do we have to take such matters into account when evaluating *My Bed* artistically and aesthetically? What would it matter to our understanding of the artwork if her biography ultimately proved to be an invention?

When writing about a living artist, it is impossible to ignore the creative person and the persona he or she chooses to project. Whether we like it or not, we continue to live with the Romantic legacy of the artist as a free, independent, creative, expressive subject who somehow embodies himself in his art. This was an idea explored, for example, by Tolstoy in his famous treatise on aesthetics, *What is Art?*, in which he sees the work of art as a means of communicating directly the artist's emotions to the receiver in such a way that the receiver experiences them as the creator had done. More recently, Slavoj Žižek, following on from Lacan, refers to the "presence" of the ideal or authoritative subject (of the artist) in the artwork as the "big Other".[6] Today's audiences are still fed biographical facts via programme notes, media interviews and so on, as if the only way to experience a new work of art were

---

5. These and other critical responses to *My Bed* are discussed at greater length by Cherry in ibid.
6. See, for example, Slavoj Žižek, *Looking Awry: An Introduction to Jacques Lacan Through Popular Culture* (Cambridge, MA: MIT Press, 1993). For a detailed discussion of the musical implications of this idea, see Lawrence Kramer, "The mysteries of animation: history, analysis and musical subjectivity", in: *Music Analysis* 20/ii (2001), pp. 153–78.

Jonathan Cross

LESSONS FROM THE PAST: THREE BRIEF CASE STUDIES

1. THE CASE OF IGOR STRAVINSKY

Let us consider for a moment the case of a dead composer and a still-living commentator who knew the composer intimately. The composer is Igor Stravinsky, who died in 1971, and the commentator is his long-standing assistant, friend and house guest, Robert Craft. Craft was not the first commentator to be closely associated with this composer: Arthur Lourié played a similar role in the 1920s and Stravinsky seemed always to need this kind of go-between. Craft first met Stravinsky in 1948 and, "over 23 years he shared more than 150 concerts with Stravinsky, collaborated on seven books, and conducted the world premières of a number of Stravinsky's later works."[7] In fact, he more than collaborated on those books: Craft wrote them; he shaped them; maybe he even put words into Stravinsky's mouth. He acknowledges this. Their closeness gave Craft unique insights into Stravinsky's life, but this was not without bias.

> The *Conversations* were taken down by me in informal talks. I was able to do this because for twenty-one years I lived with the Stravinskys in their Hollywood home, or in a nearby apartment, and for two more years in a next-door hotel room in New York...
>
> The *Conversations* books, unlike the ghosted *Poétique musicale* and *Chroniques de ma vie*, the pamphlets on Pushkin and Diaghilev, are the only published writings attributed to Stravinsky that are actually "by him", in the sense of fidelity to the substance of his thoughts. The language, unavoidably, is very largely mine.[8]

In fact, the books are often as much about Craft and his frequently overstated view that Stravinsky would not have achieved what he did in his later years had it not been for Craft's influence. Fascinating documents though the *Conversations* books are, they

---

7. Patrick J. Smith/Maureen Buja, "Robert Craft", *Grove Music Online*, ed. L. Macy (accessed 12 November 2003), http://www.grovemusic.com
8. Robert Craft, "Preface" to Igor Stravinsky and Robert Craft, *Memories and Commentaries* (London: Faber & Faber, 2002), p. xiii.

are decidedly unreliable as "authentic" or "truthful" accounts of Stravinsky's life, music and ideas. Who is speaking? Stravinsky or Craft? In any case, as Richard Taruskin and Stephen Walsh, among others, have shown us, Stravinsky was constantly reinventing himself, his music and his own past.[9] It is highly likely that he fed Craft lines which, given their close relationship, Craft had no option but to record as true. There could be little critical distance between composer and musicologist.[10] More than thirty years after Stravinsky's death, Craft still regards himself as the custodian of the "truth" about Stravinsky.[11] Just as what Tracey Emin tells us about her self and its relationship to her work needs to be evaluated critically, so does what Craft tells us about Stravinsky and his work.

II. THE CASE OF BENJAMIN BRITTEN

Britten is an interesting case. Here, knowledge of the composer's biography can throw fascinating interpretative light on the work. Britten was homosexual, and this impinges on many of the themes his works deal with (for example, the way he treats the relationship between the boy Miles and the dead manservant Quint in *The Turn of the Screw*; Aschenbach's obsession with the beautiful boy Tadzio in *Death in Venice*; the figure of the "outsider" in so many pieces). And yet, in his own lifetime, this issue was hardly discussed — partly, of course, because until 1967 homosexuality was still illegal in Britain — despite the fact that Britten's sexuality and his relationship with Peter Pears were a widely known "open secret", and partly because those who chose to write about Britten

---

9. See Richard Taruskin, *Stravinsky and the Russian Traditions: A Biography of the Works Through Mavra* (Oxford: Oxford University Press, 1996) and Stephen Walsh, *Igor Stravinsky: A Creative Spring: Russia and France 1882–1934* (London: Jonathan Cape, 1999).
10. For evidence of how closely the lives of Stravinsky and Craft were intertwined, see Robert Craft, *Stravinsky: Chronicle of a Friendship*, revised and expanded edition (Nashville: Vanderbilt University Press, 1994). In the plates, excluding pictures of Stravinsky's coffin, there are more images of Craft than there are of Stravinsky!
11. Craft's ill-tempered review of Walsh's biography, *Stravinsky: A Creative Spring*, is a very good case in point, where he either contests the facts presented by Walsh or else claims that Walsh merely lifted them from Craft's own works. See "Bungled biography", in: *Musical Quarterly* 85/2 (2001), pp. 391–400.

(such as Donald Mitchell) had cultivated very close relationships with him and would not write anything of which the composer would have disapproved. It took a posthumous biographer who did not know Britten personally to have the appropriate distance to deal fully and openly with these issues[12] and, in a sense, to provide a context for the recent extensive appropriation of Britten by queer theory.[13]

III. THE CASE OF DMITRI SHOSTAKOVICH

It is impossible to believe very much Shostakovich said about himself. Under the Soviet regime, Shostakovich had to lie to survive. As David Fanning, among others, has demonstrated,[14] there is no testimony about the composer — not even the protestations of his own son — that can be claimed to be necessarily true or authentic. In his discussion of the Eighth String Quartet, Fanning tries to avoid reading the work as a kind of encoded autobiography, resisting the highly attractive power of Shostakovich's own confession that, while composing the quartet, "in memory of myself ... my tears flowed as abundantly as urine after downing half a dozen beers."[15] Because such a statement, even in a letter, is so unreliable, Fanning turns to the formal concerns of "the music itself" and claims authenticity through reference to newly available sketch material. Do these documents posthumously reveal the "truth" that the composer in his lifetime was unable to tell? Do they now tell us things that musicologists working when he was alive could not have known? Even here the problem for Fanning is that the material is still very incomplete. There is, then, a very real danger of mapping life onto art when the veracity of what we know about that life is so totally uncertain. Or, to put it a rather different way, what the composer intended and what we hear are two completely

---

12. Humphrey Carpenter, *Benjamin Britten: A Biography* (London: Faber & Faber, 1992).
13. An excellent example of such writing is Philip Brett, "Eros and orientalism in Britten's operas", in Philip Brett, Elizabeth Wood & Gary C. Thomas (eds.), *Queering the Pitch: The New Gay and Lesbian Musicology* (Routledge: New York, 1994), pp. 235–56.
14. David Fanning, *Shostakovich: String Quartet No. 8* (Aldershot: Ashgate, 2004).
15. Letter to Isaac Glikman, 19 July 1960.

different things. This issue is particularly acute for a composer like Shostakovich whose music was consistently heard by contemporary Soviet audiences to articulate political protest. Taruskin asks: "Did the composer intend it? The question, I submit, is irrelevant... What made Shostakovich's music the secret diary of a nation was not only what he put into it, but what it allowed listeners to draw out."[16]

Similar stories can be told about many Eastern European composers (Lutosławski is a good example). Lying was a way of life under communist regimes.

THE COMPOSER SPEAKS: AN EXAMPLE FROM THE PRESENT

Birtwistle's orchestral work *The Shadow of Night* was premièred by the Cleveland Orchestra in Cleveland, Ohio, conducted by Christoph von Dohnányi, on 10 January 2002 and received its British première at the Proms in London on 12 September 2003. Uncharacteristically, the composer has given us a note about the work and its origins. This is writing, however brief, that bears the stamp of authorial authenticity. We have to take note of it because it is reproduced in the front of the published score and carries almost as much weight as the title.[17] The note tells us that *The Shadow of Night* is

> ... a slow and reflective nocturne, exploring the world of melancholy as understood and celebrated by Elizabethan poets and composers.
>
> The title is drawn form a long poem by George Chapman (1559–1634), which is one of the fullest explorations of this theme, where melancholy is no longer an inert and depressive mood, but a humour of the night, an inspired spiritual condition.

---

16. Richard Taruskin, "Shostakovich and us", in Rosamund Bartlett (ed.), *Shostakovich in Context* (Oxford: Oxford University Press, 2000), p. 5 & 7.
17. In fact, the composer's words carry such authority that a major error of fact is transmitted in this note, unchecked by the publisher: the note claims that *Earth Dances* was also written for the Cleveland Orchestra when it was actually a BBC commission.

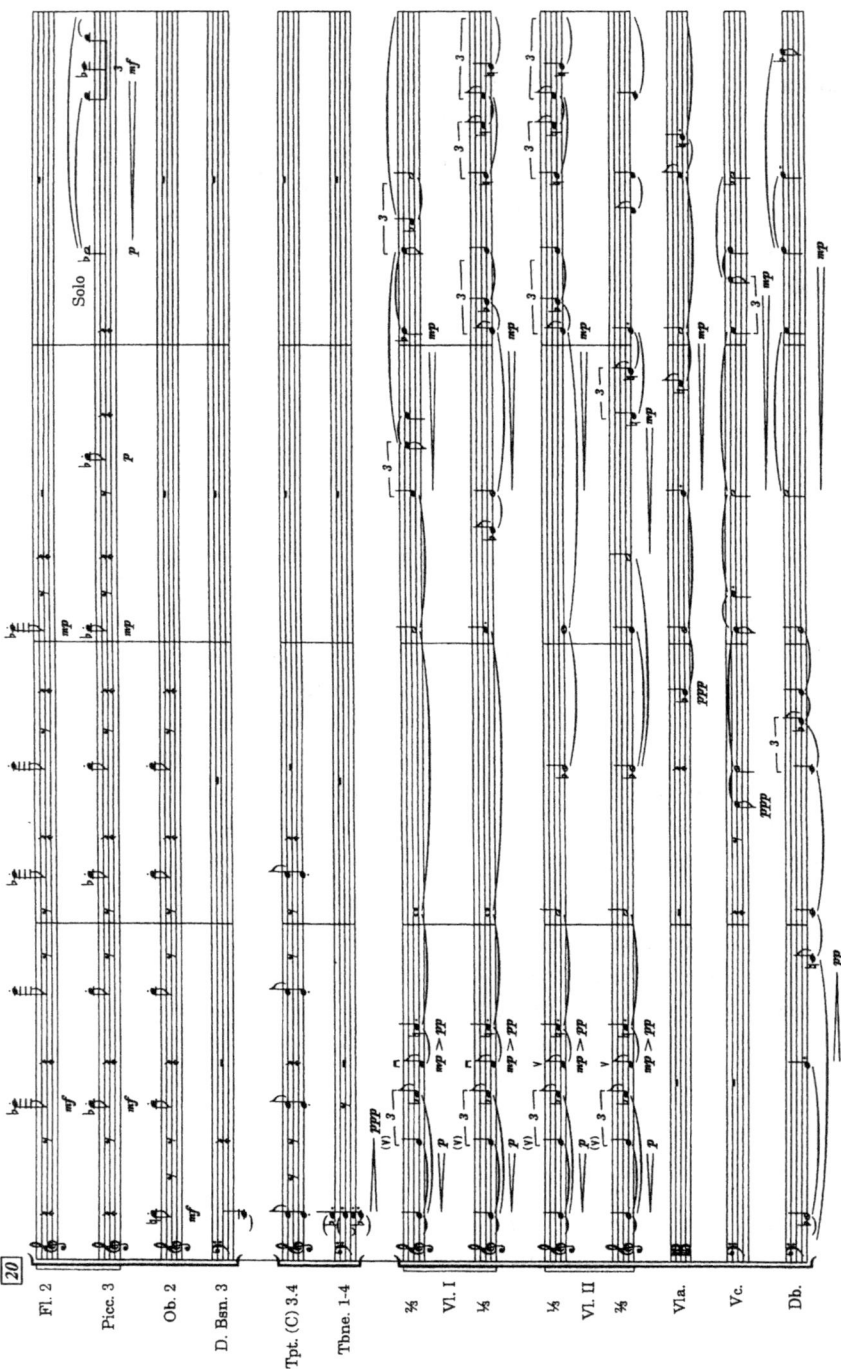

Ex. 1 Birtwistle, *The Shadow of Night*, bars 20–24: "Dowland motif" (piccolo solo).
© 2003 by Boosey & Hawkes Music Publishers Ltd. Reproduced by kind permission of Boosey & Hawkes Music Publishers Ltd.

I took inspiration from two dark sources — the expressions of melancholy in Albrecht Dürer's engraving *Melencolia I* (1514) and John Dowland's lute song *In Darkness Let Me Dwell*, the first three notes of which are quoted in the piccolo's solo soon after the opening of the piece. This motif, which rises a semitone and down again, is woven into the fabric of the work and also alluded to figuratively: lines split and later reunite, the notes of a chord move away and back again, and longer melodic lines are interrupted and resumed like the moon shining through a series of slowly passing clouds.

Ex. 1 shows the moment where the "Dowland motif" first appears in the piccolo. With the score in front of us, we can quickly see — as the composer asserts — that this motif occurs frequently throughout the piece. Any writer would want to take account of this. But I wonder if we would give it quite this prominence if the composer had not chosen to drawn our attention to it? Without his note, would it have been possible to relate a rising then falling semitone directly to Dowland? Even with the note, do we hear this in any way related to Dowland's song? I suspect not. The falling semitone, as a topic of grief, has evident connections with melancholy. But its source could come from anywhere in European art music over the past 500 years or more. More specifically, it is the kind of musical idea that occurs — either literally or in related gestures such as a rising semitone then a falling tone — in very many of Birtwistle's works.

Nonetheless, many of the writers connected with the London première of *The Shadow of Night* loyally followed Birtwistle's lead. The Proms programme book note by David Beard describes this three-note figure as "a central idea" that pervades the work. Andrew Clements, reviewing the performance in the *Guardian* newspaper, mentions "the opening of a Dowland lute song as a thematic germ;" Hilary Finch, reviewing it for *The Times*, talks of "its musical seeds, a tiny rising and falling semitone, ... scattered from Dowland's ayre *In darkness let me dwell.*" None of them is willing to question the truth or significance of the composer's observation: it carries unquestioned authority. But I wonder how important this motif was for the listeners in the hall or the readers of the reviews?

It seems to me that all these writers are using this idea not just because it carries the aura of the composer with it. The rhetoric of "central ideas", "germs" and "seeds" also alludes to the language of music analysis, specifically Schoenberg-style motivic analysis, grounded in notions of organic unity, musical logic and coherence. These writers are implicitly suggesting that this is important music because it can be analysed in a way that relates it to the great music of the musical past. I have more to say below about the connections between cultural value and music that is "analysable".

I had the privilege to interview Birtwistle in public in the Royal Albert Hall before the Proms performance. I have interviewed him many times before and we have developed a good working relationship: we trust one another, in that he knows I won't ask him questions he won't be able to answer, and I know that he won't refuse to speak and leave me "high and dry". Clearly, then, when I am with the composer, I have to behave quite differently from the way I behave as a musicologist sat at my desk. I have to relinquish some of my critical distance. But this is merely to recognise (as perhaps some of the writers above did not) that the occasion, the medium and the audience influence what we say. A composer interview does very different things from a piece of criticism.

I asked Birtwistle about the quotation from another melancholic Elizabethan lute song, John Danyel's *Can Doleful Notes*, that appears on page 39 of the score. It is the first time such a text has appeared in any of his scores. Who is it for? The conductor? The analyst? Clearly it is not for the players (the quotation does not appear in the parts) or for the listener. Its relationship to the actual music is as non-specific as the relationship between the three-note motif and Dowland's song. Having studied the score in detail and thought about this moment a great deal before the interview, I eventually asked the composer why it occurs where it does. His answer was a surprise. He claimed that it was because that was the moment he had reached in the composition of the score when he happened to stumble across the Danyel poem. He therefore just wrote it into the score at that point. It has no direct connection with the music. Do we believe him? Is it right to question the veracity of a composer's statements? Without this information, we would be trying to relate text to context. With it, the situation is more complicated.

WORK IN PROGRESS: AN OEUVRE IN THE MAKING

All those of us who write about living composers are perpetually aware of the fact that the ground is constantly shifting beneath our feet (a kind of musicological "earth dance", you might say). This clearly makes writing about living composers different from writing about dead composers. Anything we say has a provisional status. This is both the challenge and the excitement about working in this area. No-one has written about this music before. We have to take risks and what we say may in the long run prove to be wrong. Little wonder, then, that many cling to the life-belt of the composer's own words in order to lend an aura of authenticity to what they say.

1. HARRISON BIRTWISTLE

How does *The Shadow of Night* affect the way we think about Birtwistle's earlier works? Clearly it must — any new work changes the picture of the whole. Birtwistle says it is a companion piece to *Earth Dances*. But *Earth Dances* was itself a "companion" to *Secret Theatre*. The composer is also describing *Night's Black Bird* as a companion piece to *The Shadow of Night*.[18] This work, too, is sure to change our view of *Earth Dances*, as well as of *The Shadow of Night*. But how? How does *Shadow* make us look back at *Earth Dances* in new ways? Birtwistle says it is a work concerned with exploring melancholy, and he articulates this idea much more explicitly than he has done in the past. How then does this invite us to re-evaluate *all* his earlier works in the light of this theme? *Melencolia I* (1976), in particular, draws on the same materials (such as Dürer's etching). How does *Shadow of Night* change the way we think about *Melencolia I*? There is no space here to explore all these questions, but I would suggest that the way in which musical ideas are layered in all these works may, in the light of

---

18. At the time of writing, Birtwistle was still composing *Night's Black Bird*. It was a commission by the Lucerne Festival for the Cleveland Orchestra, conducted by Franz Welser-Möst, and received its world première on 21 August 2004.

the notion of melancholy, open a number of interpretative possibilities. The continually shifting relationship between linear (melodic, "cantus") and repeating (ostinato, "continuum") ideas is common to them all. In relation to *Melencolia I*, Birtwistle quoted Günter Grass's essay, "On stasis in progress: variations on Albrecht Dürer's *Melencolia I*",[19] and this continues to stand as an apt metaphor for his musical processes. While the linearity of the clarinet's "sad song" in *Melencolia I* was an important feature of that work, progress/continuity is, arguably, more central to *Shadow*. Yet a sense of (melancholic) stasis is, paradoxically, all the stronger in the recent piece. The recent work invites us to re-evaluate the relationship between "cantus" and "continuum" (themselves terms derived from the later *Secret Theatre*) in the earlier work, and to reassess the priority given to one over the other. I would also suggest that the composer's explicit invocation of an *English* tradition in *The Shadow of Night* (Elizabethan melancholic verse and song) makes us look afresh at the kind of national identity, of "musical Englishness", that is being (unconsciously) constructed even in *Melencolia I*.

II. PIERRE BOULEZ

Boulez's work in progress offers an extreme example. How can we discuss — let alone analyse — a work that is in the public domain (in different versions) yet which is known to be incomplete? Take *Répons*, begun in 1981. Writing in 1984, the French musicologist Dominique Jameux commented:

> ... the work I am describing is still (1984) unfinished. *Répons 2* is equal to about half the projected length of the complete work ... This incompleteness ... necessarily distorts perspective. *Répons 2* — with its present "coda" perfectly balancing the purely instrumental introduction and its two huge "durational effects" — therefore presents a formal achievement which is in fact an illusion.[20]

---

19. Günter Grass, *From the Diary of a Snail*, trans. Ralph Manheim (London: Minerva, 1997). First published as *Aus dem Tagebuch einer Schnecke* in 1972.
20. Dominique Jameux, *Pierre Boulez*, trans. Susan Bradshaw (London: Faber & Faber, 1991), p. 364.

Répons 1 ended with what Jameux calls the "funeral march" section, after about 19'30". The "finale" (Jameux's designation) up to *c.* 29' is "only a provisional ending. However, with the work in its present state, this huge and somewhat uniform crescendo ... clearly gives the impression of fulfilling this function."[21] The "coda" is as provisional as the preceding "finale", "even though its coda-like character is fairly clear."[22] When an ending turns out not to be an ending, the usefulness of the critical apparatus we rely on to understand such music is seriously called into question. Perhaps we also ought to be more explicit about acknowledging that, like Boulez's music, our musicology is provisional and "in progress"?

Arnold Whittall has attempted a brief analysis of *Sur Incises* of 1996–8, itself an elaborate reworking of *Incises* of 1994. He quotes what he calls "Boulez's Debussian self-analysis: 'I need, or work with, a lot of accidents, but within a structure that has an overall trajectory — and that, for me, is the definition of what is organic'."[23] This is an interesting move on Boulez's part: no longer the enfant terrible, he is trying to integrate his avant-garde tendencies within the analytical mainstream by invoking tried-and-tested (and, of course, loaded) categories such as organicism. Whittall glosses the comment as follows: "Boulez's IRCAM works embody precisely this shift of emphasis in favour of the organic, which gives new strength to classicising aspirations to integration, and moves the kind of modernistic tension he once celebrated in Berg to the margins."[24] Present practice is differentiated from past practice. But also past practice needs to be understood in the light of present practice. How do we now interpret the radicalism of, say, his mobile form pieces of the 1950s in the context of his more recent retreat into organicism? Maybe the third piano sonata was less radical than Boulez's polemics of the time had led us to

---

21. ibid., p. 366.
22. ibid., p. 367.
23. Arnold Whittall, *Exploring Twentieth-Century Music: Tradition and Innovation* (Cambridge: Cambridge University Press, 2003), p. 191. Whittall is quoting from Rocco di Pietro, *Dialogues with Boulez* (Lanham, MD: Scarecrow Press, 2001), p. 25.
24. Whittall, ibid.

believe? His recent comments invite us to look again at the post-War avant-garde in terms of continuities with, rather than breaks from, the past.

III. MICHAEL FINNISSY

Michael Finnissy is often grouped with figures such as Brian Ferneyhough, James Dillon and Richard Barrett under the heading of "complexity". But what does such a label mean, and how does it influence the way in which this music is received? Ferneyhough has written:

> It would be nice to abandon the use of the term "complex" ... since there is little communality of intent or aesthetic position discernible beyond the number of note heads per page... "Complexity" needs to be seen more as a *terminus technicus* and less as a convenient blanket term for a style or school.[25]

Elsewhere he has spoken of:

> ... the entire constellation of confusion surrounding the term "complex" itself. One senses here a desire to bring to the surface certain long-repressed, unconscious fears of chaos which society has chosen to ignore, to express, analyze and re-animate those taboos as opposition to the pernicious spread of bland, media-influenced "good common sense" symbolism, aimed at manipulating other, equally unspoken drives in the name of convenience and commercial profit. The characteristic and deliberately prodigal expenditure of musical invention and formal ambition (not to mention performer effort) is a completely valid attempt to confront this conspiracy of silence head-on.[26]

Ferneyhough pulls no punches there. But it does highlight the problems of the ways in which a term, coined by critics and loosely applied, can be highly misleading and may seriously

---

25. Brian Ferneyhough, "Response to a questionnaire on 'complexity'", in: *Collected Writings*, ed. James Boros & Richard Toop (Amsterdam: Harwood Academic Press, 1995), p. 67.
26. Ferneyhough, "Interview with Antonio De Lisa", in: *Collected Writings*, p. 425.

Ex. 2 Finnissy, *English Country-Tunes*, "Come beat the drums and sound the fifes" (excerpt).
Reproduced by kind permission of United Music Publishers Ltd.

Ex. 3 Finnissy, *The Cambridge Codex* (excerpt).
© Oxford University Press

prejudice the possibility of access to the work of living composers. Critics and musicologists do create constraining frames within which the new is received. Finnissy denies his music is complex ... and perhaps with good reason. Exx. 2 and 3 show excerpts from two of Finnissy's works produced twenty years apart. The rhythmic and harmonic density of the first, "Come beat the drums and sound the fifes" from *English Country-Tunes* (1977) for piano solo, might legitimately be understood as complex; the modal simplicity of the second, a passage from *The Cambridge Codex* (1991) for mezzo soprano, flute, violin, cello and bells, does not, at first glance, look as if it could have been written by the same composer. It therefore must throw interesting light back on the earlier work.

What does this later simplicity tell us about Finnissy's earlier complexity? I think we *do* now judge his earlier music in a very different way. A closer examination of these two examples reveals that the composer is treating the material in similar ways by means of rhythmic variation and a kind of cycling round certain pitch fields ("modes"). That the surface of the two pieces seems "complex" or "simple" is not really the issue here: the labels merely exaggerate the obvious differences and hide the similarities. Finnissy's music is saying interesting things about our attitude to musical style and the expectations styles bring with them. Style is irrelevant: he is able to draw on music from all over the world and incorporate it into his own compositions, the results being (often) stylistically eclectic but compositionally consistent.

CANON FORMATION

What does the canon mean to living composers? Does the notion of a canon still have a function in the twenty-first century? There are differing views.

The idea of a canon of "great" works began to emerge in the late-eighteenth century alongside what we might now understand as an historical attitude to music. As Jim Samson writes:

> A newly consolidated bourgeois class began to define itself artistically in the late 18th century, institutionalizing its musical life in a manner independent of sacred and courtly life. It established its principal

ceremony—the public concert—in the major cities of England, France and central Europe, and it began to create a repertory of classical music, with related concert rituals, to confirm and authenticate the new status quo. By the mid-19th century it had already established much of the core repertory of the modern canon, in the process giving itself cultural roots, "inventing" tradition and creating a fetishism of the great work which is still with us today.[27]

But is this true? Do we still live with this Romantic legacy? Does it still regulate the choices we make about the music we have access to, about the value we place on certain kinds of music and not on others? Surely—thanks to the work of feminists, ethnomusicologists, popular music historians, cultural studies scholars and all those so-called "new" musicologists who have spent the last decade or more challenging autonomy and the "museum of musical works"—the very idea of a canon has been totally discredited? Paul Griffiths's history of "Many Rivers: the 1980s and 1990s" in *Modern Music and After: Directions Since 1945* would seem to suggest that, as far as the music of our own time is concerned, canon-building is an impossibility.

> The abundance of music now being written makes it hard to see the wood for the trees, the currents for the water. Perhaps in time the view will become clearer. But ... the current great number of professional composers is a new phenomenon, and one that may alter—may already have altered—the way history could extract a deposit of contemporary work for permanence. Also, time's winnowing no longer seems to be happening as it used to. Since the arrival of the compact disc, in 1982, the available repertory in all periods has vastly increased, and trends in criticism have questioned the criteria and even the value of selecting an agreed canon of masterpieces. We live now with many musical histories, and many musical presents.[28]

---

27. Jim Samson, "Canon", *Grove Music Online*, ed. L. Macy (accessed 12 November 2003), http://www.grovemusic.com
28. Paul Griffiths, *Modern Music and After: Directions since 1945* (Oxford: OUP, 1995), p. 238.

Very crudely, a postmodern climate of decentring has meant that, if the canon continues to have any validity at all, then it can only be in personal terms. We each build our own private canons, determined by our particular history, geography, ethnicity, gender, sexuality, and so on. Taste then becomes the arbiter in the choices we make about even the most recent of music. Contemporary classical music is no different from pop music. As Griffiths suggests, since the dawning of the age of the CD and, more recently, of MP-3, the unprecedented availability and accessibility of music from all times and from all over the world has inevitably changed our sense of musical and cultural values. Globalisation has had as much an impact on "classical" music as it has on the emergence of "world" music. We no longer necessarily value music "in itself" (values centred on the autonomous "abstract" instrumental music that formed the backbone of the canon); rather, we are now far more concerned with audiences and with the ways in which music is received.[29]

Yet, despite this, the fetishism of the great work that Samson identified appears to be alive and well. This is not the place to debate how and to what extent the canon of masterworks from Bach to Brahms still regulates what we see in our concert halls and opera houses, and what we hear on our radios. We are all familiar with the way in which the classical canon often serves to prevent challenging new music from being heard or taken seriously. But even within the domain of contemporary music the notion of the canon seems hard to dislodge. The "*Tempo* Masterpiece Poll",[30] shown in Ex. 4 offers clear evidence to support this. Its rhetoric of the "masterpiece" harks directly back to the process of canonisation that emerged in the nineteenth century.

In private correspondence with me, the editor of *Tempo* provided the following gloss: "I think the Masterpiece Poll COULD turn out interesting—it's not meant to be an award ceremony or

---

29. For an engaging recent discussion of the positive and negative implications of "globalisation", see Philip V. Bohlman, *World Music: A Very Short Introduction* (Oxford: Oxford University Press, 2002).
30. Calum MacDonald [Editor], "*Tempo* Masterpiece Poll", in: *Tempo* 226 (October 2003), p. 43.

TEMPO MASTERPIECE POLL

> Nothing is likely about masterpieces, least of all whether there will be any.
> – Stravinsky in conversation with Robert Craft, 1957

So if 'the ruling class won't pay up, how is a large proportion of the population even going to hear a new masterpiece, let alone recognise it?'. In the interim, it would seem that '... the emergence of new masterpieces ...recognized as such', can only begin with the recognition of such works by individuals, in advance of any 'large proportion of the population'. The Johnson/Silverman correspondence prompts *Tempo* to announce its very own 'Masterpiece Poll', in an attempt to identify whether such phenomena continue to appear, whether any proportion of us continue to believe that they are appearing, and whether there may exist any consensus in identifying them. Accordingly we invite any and all readers of *Tempo* to name one contemporary work to which they would unhesitatingly accord the rank of masterpiece.

The editorship of Tempo suggests this exercise in the full knowledge that there will be readers who regard the whole concept of the 'masterpiece' as deeply unhelpful, elitist or perhaps offensive, not to say irrelevant to today's culture – even that tiny sector of the culture described by terms like 'contemporary classical music'. On the other hand, most of us use the appellation 'masterpiece' at some time or other; and most of us think we know, more or less, what we mean by it.

While not seeking to limit choice in any way, here are a few guidelines:

1. Each reader may only nominate one musical work. There are no restrictions on nationality of composer or on genre, ensemble or idiom, as long as the work nominated is recognizable as 'contemporary classical music', but it must have been composed or at least completed in the last quarter-century, ie no earlier than 1977. Works written before that date but not *premièred* until after it will not qualify.
2. Proposals should stem from personal conviction: i.e. even if the nominator has professional musical standing he or she writes, in this case, as 'enthusiastic amateur'.
3. The work proposed should be a piece which the proposer feels has brought new things into his/her life, which he/she will be happy to hear again many times, and wants to share with other music-lovers. It will be assumed the proposer has heard the work at least once unless the piece is unperformed/unrecorded and the proposer has come to their very high opinion of it on a reading of the score only; in which case this should be stated in the nomination.
4. Proposers may not nominate their own works.
5. Proposals should be in the form of the title and composer of the work, accompanied by a maximum of two sentences justifying the choice: ie a brief description of the work, indicating where you think or feel its excellence lies. Perceived failings or flaws may also be mentioned (not all masterpieces of the past are flawless). For this aspect alone a third sentence will be allowed. No profile of the composer need be given, as the emphasis should be on the chosen work. Should the editor require further information, he will ask. If the work is commercially recorded, please give details; if there are multiple recordings, give details only of your preferred version.
6. Proposals may be e-mailed to macval@compuserve.com, faxed to (44) 01453 821575 or posted to the *Tempo* editorial address, P.O. Box 171, Herne Bay, Kent CT6 6WD.
7. The closing date for nominations will be 1 June 2004 and the results of the poll will be printed in Tempo Volume 58, No.230 (October 2004 issue).
8. There are no prizes: not even for the composer of the most-often nominated work, if any should chance to be nominated more than once. The nominations are rewards in themselves. All works nominated will be listed, with the number of proposals for each and such editorial commentary as the results seem to call for. The most impressive, enlightening, entertaining or otherwise self-recommending justificatory texts will be published: the choice of these will be the Editor's and will be final.

Calum MacDonald
Editor, TEMPO

Ex. 4 TEMPO

even a '100 best', but just to see what people will actually stick their necks out for when they can only name ONE piece. It occurs to me I should perhaps have promised all those nominating that they'll have anonymity if they want it — imagine all the music journalists who could rapidly lose a lot of composer-friends!"[31] I remain to be convinced of the value of such an exercise. Surely what will emerge is, if not a "100 best", then at least a top ten. And what will that tell us? The notion of the masterpiece implicitly carries with it — does it not? — values of seriousness, longevity/permanence in the repertoire (and in notation?), craftsmanship (the equivalent of "painterly" qualities in the visual arts), a certain scale, and so on. It is more likely that, say, Messiaen's opera *Saint François d'Assise* is going to appear on this list[32] than, say, Rebecca Saunders's *chroma* prepared for the vast Turbine Hall of Tate Modern, which required the "listener" to move around the installation ("You have to mix the music with your feet", wrote the composer). But what makes one piece any more "masterful" than another? The way in which, throughout the twentieth century and into the twenty-first, the boundaries of the musical artwork (physically, aurally, performatively, geographically) have been expanded and challenged would seem to make the values of the masterwork redundant, not to mention the patriarchal and imperial implications of the term *master*. Yet the desire to reaffirm these bourgeois values appears to be as strong as ever.

The role of a journal such as *Tempo* in forming opinion about contemporary music — in defining a canon of works as art — is itself an interesting one. To return to Samson's *New Grove* article:

> This process of canon formation was aided, moreover, by taste-creating institutions such as journals and publishing houses. The history of the *Revue et Gazette musicale* is indicative. So too is the series of collected editions produced by Breitkopf & Härtel in the late 19th century.

---

31. Private email correspondence, 14 November 2003.
32. A work whose transcendental nature was recently praised by Richard Taruskin as representing the "quest for the uncanny otherness of the eternal" (p. 119) and "affording glimpses of other worlds and other minds" (p. 126). See "Sacred entertainments", in: *Cambridge Opera Journal* 15/2 (2003), pp. 109–26.

I would argue that it is still true today that the opinions of a journal editor in selecting and commissioning articles on particular composers and kinds of repertoire (and not others) are therefore highly influential. Similarly the role of publishing directors at the major music publishers today and the role of senior producers with radio stations and CD labels are equally influential. To take again the example of Birtwistle, it is worth noting that two of his works from the mid-1980s — *Secret Theatre* (1984) and *Earth Dances* (1985–6) — have been recorded three times each, and in the case of *Earth Dances* by such distinguished figures as Eötvös, Dohnányi and Boulez. Why does a company of the standing of Deutsche Grammophon, who released the Boulez recording coupled with a new work, *Theseus Game*, in 2004, choose to return to "old" repertoire, when there are so many important works by exciting living composers that are not widely available on commercial CDs? It seems to me that there is a kind of canon formation taking place here, but one driven primarily by commercial values. *Earth Dances* is thus accorded the status of a "masterpiece". It should hardly surprise us that it is an "abstract" orchestral work on a vast scale that easily corresponds with the "heroic" model of the masterwork established by Beethoven's symphonies in key nineteenth-century writings, such as those of Adolf Bernhard Marx.

The issue of *Tempo*, to which I have already referred, devotes two of its four main articles to the work of the living British composer Robin Holloway, who celebrated his sixtieth birthday in 2003. This fact in itself shows the editor sending out a signal: here is a composer worthy of our attention. This is all the more interesting in the light of the comments made in the articles. The first is an interview with the composer himself. Prompted by his interviewer to comment on an earlier view about "censorship" in contemporary music he observes:

> I feel almost completely out of it. I'm very little played, given my age, as compared obviously to the minimalists ... The BBC has deemed a "Composer of the Week" inappropriate. You'd think my attempt to open up forbidden and active territory would be appealing... I don't think I have any clout at all in what's left of modern music circles... The pigeon-holes

and mental compartments are all the more confining these days for not being spoken. The invisible censors are more powerful than ever.[33]

Who are these "invisible censors"? Holloway evidently believes there to be some sort of canon in operation (hence his comment about the minimalists) which discriminates against his (old-fashioned?) brand of modernism. And he appears to subscribe to a conspiracy theory with regard to the way in which the contemporary canon is formed.

The next article in this issue of *Tempo*—written by Anthony Gritten, a young British musicologist with a position at a respectable English university—is essentially analytical in perspective, dedicated to an examination of one work, Holloway's *Showpiece*, premièred and published (by Boosey & Hawkes) in 1983. Again, the author is here concerned with the apparent neglect of a work he considers to be of great value. The reason he gives for this neglect is a rather different one from that given by the composer. Unlike much music of our century (he lists works by Schoenberg, Birtwistle, Tippett, Reich, Bartók, Boulez, Stockhausen, Goehr and Stravinsky), *Showpiece* does not lend itself to musical analysis.

> Music analysis ... has often been taken ... to be something of a midwife to contemporary music. The labour of music (taking this term in both its economic and its procreative sense) is guided, constrained, manipulated, liberated—by analysis. Music analysis acts upon musical works to provide a form of cultural capital for society. It is the cowboy staking claim in the far West to the cultural homesteaders back East, the soldier to the businessman.
>
> Robin Holloway's *Showpiece* is not one of these works: it neither repels nor attracts analysis.[34]

So it is the *music analyst* who is acting as the invisible censor. Is there any truth in this, especially in an era when—at least in the English-speaking world—the analyst has come under sustained

---

33. Ivan Hewett, "Composer in interview: Robin Holloway", in: *Tempo* 226 (October 2003), p. 18.
34. Anthony Gritten, "Robin Holloway's 'Showpiece'", in: *Tempo* 226 (October 2003), p. 21.

attack for continuing to promote formalist musical values?[35] One of the reasons Schoenberg's twelve-note music so quickly achieved canonical status was because its compositional processes were analysable, and could therefore have a relatively straightforward place in university and conservatoire curricula. Stravinsky did not reveal his secrets so easily. Once Adorno had mapped a *rational developmental subjectivity* on to Schoenberg and a *primitive non-developmental objectivity* on to Stravinsky, and then promulgated these values via such key post-War opinion-forming institutions as the Darmstadt Ferienkurse für Neue Musik, the values of another generation of composers were sealed. Just look at the influence Boulez and Stockhausen still exert on contemporary music, in part reinforced by their representation through the "powerhouse" of mid-century music publishing, Universal Edition. Schoenberg's emigration to the USA and (unlike Stravinsky) his rapid appointment to positions within the academy, meant that it was perhaps inevitable that his approach to serialism was going to be more highly valued than other methods or ideas. At a time (after the Second World War) when the humanities in American universities were fighting for funding, the pseudo-scientific ideology of serialism and its reception by the likes of Babbitt and his followers at Princeton was more than likely to be preferred over more "expressive" or "instinctive" musics. The professionalisation of American music theory meant turning it into a "natural science" — witness the work of Allen Forte at Yale and the value he places, through pitch-class set theory, on the music of Schoenberg. The title of his celebrated article, "The magical kaleidoscope: Schoenberg's first atonal masterwork, Opus 11, No. 1",[36] tells us much about the canonical status afforded Schoenberg's music. So maybe there is a nugget of truth in Gritten's argument. The institutions of musicology (and I call music analysis one of these) play their part in framing the reception of new music.

---

35. For insight into the arguments — at least, in North America — between the "formalists" and the "contextualists", see Pieter C. van den Toorn, "In defense of music theory", in: *Music, Politics, and the Academy* (Berkeley: University of California Press, 1995), pp. 44–64.
36. *Journal of the Arnold Schoenberg Institute* 5 (1981), pp. 127–68.

Book publishing, too, plays a role in forming opinion about new work. In the space of eighteen months between 1998 and 2000, no fewer than three books on the music of Harrison Birtwistle had appeared, along with a major dissertation on the early works.[37] Quite a phenomenon. Why did Birtwistle merit this coverage? Is his music self-evidently so much "better" than that of countless other composers, so much more "masterly"? Why has not the music of other British composers of a similar vintage enjoyed equal attention? There are no books — let alone three — on Nicholas Maw, Thea Musgrave or David Bedford, to pluck some names at random of composers who are published by major houses and who enjoy a reasonable international profile through performances and broadcasts.

But then again, perhaps it is not such a difficult question to answer. The music of Maw, while espousing modern values, was never part of that more progressive avant-garde school associated with Manchester in the 1950s (Birtwistle, Goehr, Maxwell Davies), and allied himself to a nineteenth-century symphonic tradition that has earned him — unfairly, in my view — the perception of being "conservative". Musgrave has lived much of her later life in North America and is also a woman — two reasons perhaps, to recap Holloway's words, she has lacked "clout" in "modern music circles". A double whammy. And Bedford — a leading experimentalist figure of the 1960s — has turned his attention to community and educational projects, again distancing himself from the opinion-forming centre. Why should writing good music for school orchestras be deemed less significant than writing good music for the BBC Symphony Orchestra? In many respects, of course, it is more important. But that is not how canons are formed. Birtwistle, meanwhile, continues to receive strings of prestigious commissions from high-profile organisations inside and beyond

---

37. Robert Adlington, *The Music of Harrison Birtwistle* (Cambridge: Cambridge University Press, 2000); David Beard, "An analysis and sketch study of Harrison Birtwistle's early instrumental works (*c.* 1957–77)", D.Phil. dissertation, University of Oxford (1999); Jonathan Cross, *Harrison Birtwistle: Man, Mind, Music* (London: Faber & Faber, 2000); Michael Hall, *Harrison Birtwistle in Recent Years* (London: Robson, 1998), the successor to Hall's *Harrison Birtwistle* (London: Robson, 1984).

the UK. Both Adlington's and my books pick out common themes from the music (theatre, melody, text, temporality) that align Birtwistle's brand of modernism with earlier canonical values and underpin his original creative voice. Both — loosely speaking — take an analytical approach. Beard's and Hall's studies give further institutional credibility to the music (and, by implication to their own writing) by engaging in that highly respectable musicological activity of sketch study. Formalism and positivism thus give credence to the music being studied. And only certain kinds of music are susceptible to such discussion.

Musicologists, then, are not just objective commentators. In the choices we make with regard to the music we think appropriate for study, the methodologies we adopt, the contexts within which we present our ideas and the institutions that support the dissemination of these materials — all these factors have an influence on the way in which the music of living composers is commissioned, promoted and received. We need to be aware of our responsibilities.

But, having said that, I believe that such musicological work is none the less crucial. There is an interesting symbiotic relationship between composer and musicologist — each depends on the other (though composers would probably not admit it). As Alastair Williams puts it, "music is embedded in discourses and surrounded by ideas that contribute to its meaning. Musicology, therefore, is as old as music: you cannot have one without the other."[38] The musicologist creates a climate in which new ideas can be understood. It is a nonsense to say that a new music can speak for itself. Even before a note of it has been heard, a context is created by publishers' publicity (sometimes written by musicologists), newspaper pre-performance articles and interviews, programme notes (again often the province of musicologists), the published score, even the title of a piece. A book such as mine on Birtwistle — I hope — offers contexts within which newer works by this composer can also be made sense of. It offers listening strategies which, when composers are not necessarily working within a received tradition (such as — most obviously — tonality),

---

38. Alastair Williams, *Constructing Musicology* (Aldershot: Ashgate, 2001), p. 1.

enables audiences to orientate themselves within a new work, and to situate that work within a broader context of contemporary musical practice. These are grand claims. But the evangelist in me likes to believe that I am bringing new music to wider audiences and enriching their listening experience. And — to return to my earlier point — the musicologist does not need to be in the pocket of the composer, or to be seen as the composer's spokesperson, in order to achieve this.

THE CRITICS

Musicological writing is not the only kind of work that influences the reception of new music. Criticism, too, plays a key role in helping new works into the world (more midwifery!) ... a role, it is interesting to note, that is often played by musicologists, raising questions about where the boundaries lie between musicology, analysis and criticism. The work of the critic is not universally respected. One of the most polemical attacks on criticism was written by Hans Keller (himself a sometime critic) who described it as "the most self-evident phoney profession since witch-pricking." He was happy to assert as an ideal that "the critic was, or should be, a bridge between the composer and the listener, a bridge all the more necessary at a time when there was an inevitable cleft, if not an abyss, between the contemporary composer and his potential audience." Unfortunately, Keller's experience of what he regarded as seriously flawed criticisms of the music of Schoenberg and Britten (both of whose music he respected deeply) led him to the view that, in general, critics did the opposite of bridge-building: "criticism has put obstacles in the way of understanding."[39]

Critics, one would imagine, strive to maintain their critical independence. They would surely be discredited as critics if they were seen arbitrarily to promote the interests of one composer over another. But remember what Calum MacDonald wrote: "...imagine all the music journalists who could rapidly lose a lot

---

39. Hans Keller, *Criticism* (London: Faber & Faber, 1987), p. 30 & 34.

of composer-friends" if their cover was blown in relation to the *Tempo* Poll. Composer-friends? How can you be friendly with those whose music you criticise? Recall the case of Robert Craft. Maybe those critics are not striving to be as objective as we thought they were. They have their agendas, as do the editors of the newspapers that publish their reviews.

To test these observations, I wish to look more closely at the critical response to a work by Birtwistle entitled *Panic*. Scored for wind orchestra, saxophone and drums, it was commissioned for the Last Night of the Centenary Proms Season in 1995. Its title refers, ostensibly, to the Greek god Pan, represented by the rebellious solo saxophone, but the work also sponsored a certain "panic" amongst audience and critics. The "moral outrage" that the performance engendered was, at least in part, a result of the programming—the second half of the Last Night is traditionally the occasion for end-of-term frolics and rousing, patriotic tunes. Loud, seemingly unmelodic, hard-hitting modernist music was seen to be unsettling, offensive even, to the petty bourgeoisie who usually enjoy these closing festivities each year.

Despite the big build-up the piece had been given by the press in the run-up to the première, *Panic* did not immediately prompt the kind of riot sparked by the first performance of *The Rite of Spring*. In fact, applause in the Royal Albert Hall was polite, albeit subdued. The BBC telephone switchboard, however, was jammed with calls from angry viewers (it had been broadcast live on BBC1, the main BBC TV channel). The real riot came during the following days in the national press. Opinion was sharply divided along a line we might crudely call the tabloid–broadsheet axis. The popular press wrote of:

> ... unmitigated rubbish. An absolutely horrible noise... (*Daily Express*)
> ... last fright of the Proms ... (*Today*)

Richard Littlejohn, famous for his polemics in the *Sun* and other tabloids, wrote of:

> an atrocity of epic proportions. It was like sitting down for a dinner in a reliable restaurant and being presented with an hors d'oeuvre of cold sick ... I should be amazed if *Panic* is ever performed in public again [it

has been, many times], let alone committed to compact disc [it was released within a year by Decca[40]]... [It] is the aural equivalent of Gilbert and George, whose current exhibition, *Naked Shit*, features the artists surrounded by their own faeces and baring their backsides to the camera. (*The Spectator*)

The broadsheets took a completely different view:

> ... exhilarating... it reached the soul of the saxophone and revealed wonders only Birtwistle could have found ... (*Daily Telegraph*)
> ... it was utterly, utterly marvellous ... (*Observer*)
> ... brief, magical breaths of wind music ... (*The Times*)

What was going on here? Why did *Panic* generate such opposing reactions? How much did it have to do with "the music itself"? And to what extent were these critics' verdicts merely a matter of "taste"? Julian Johnson, in his recent book *Who Needs Classical Music?* has tackled this issue head on. "During the last few decades", he writes, "most cultural critics have come to agree that the division between 'high' and 'low' art is an artificial one, that Beethoven's Ninth and 'Blue Suede Shoes' are equally valuable as cultural texts." Or, one might say, in the context of the 1995 Last Night, that there was an inversion of canonical values in evidence where a set of slight but pleasing musical numbers by Henry Wood (namely the *Fantasia on British Sea-Songs* that has been played at the Last Night for many decades) was preferred over *Panic*, the serious product of the imagination of one of Britain's leading living composers. Johnson does not balk at reasserting modern (as opposed to postmodern) values. Music, he argues "is more than just 'a matter of taste': while some music provides entertainment, or serves as background noise, other music claims to function as art."[41]

---

40. Recorded by the same performers as gave the Proms première: John Harle (saxophone), Paul Clarvis (drum kit), BBC Symphony Orchestra, conducted by Andrew Davis (London: Decca, 1996), 452 104–2. It is coupled with the interpretation of *Earth Dances*, discussed above, by the Cleveland Orchestra, conducted by Christoph von Dohnányi.
41. Julian Johnson, *Who Needs Classical Music?* (New York: Oxford University Press, 2002), cover blurb.

Birtwistle described *Panic* as a "dithyramb", a song, a wild choral dance, for the god Pan, that disreputable Arcadian god with "horns, beard, tail and goat-legs"[42] who would revenge himself on those who disturbed him with a sudden loud shout from a grove which made the hair bristle on their heads (in panic).[43] Pan was primitive, uncultured, phallic. And Pan loved riot,[44] so there is certain poetic justice in the reaction to *Panic*. Of course, Pan's values are not those of the pseudo-Victorian petty bourgeoisie present at the Proms. And in "representing" Pan, *Panic*, too, contests those values that make for "good" music as established by the tonal canon: rhythm is given priority over melody; repetition, ostinato and local pedal points are given priority over sustained development; local sonic effect, instrumental dialogue and immediate climax are given priority over larger-scale structural design. An alternative set of values is asserted.

What is interesting here is the role the press played (on both sides) in sustaining certain prejudices about "difficult" or "elitist" modern music. Clearly those aspects of this music which might be taken to offend (in the context of the Last Night) have been played up. This was, at the very least, music of *bad taste*. But in fact what we see happening is the press playing games. There are no absolute values here of right or wrong, good or bad. The critics are behaving precisely as their editors expect them to in relation to their target audience. Their language exposes them. One man's "horrible noise" is another's "magical breaths".

Others were playing games with *Panic* too. The BBC is clearly implicated. John Drummond, for whom 1995 was his last season as Proms Director, made a wilful act of provocation by commissioning a modernist work for the second half of the Last Night. And what of Birtwistle himself? He regularly displays a general disregard for his audience: "I can't consider anything to do with who listens [to my music]," he once declared in a radio interview. He claims he just wrote for the Proms the kind of music he always

---

42. Robert Graves, *The Greek Myths* [Combined Edition] (London: Penguin, 1992), p. 101.
43. ibid.
44. ibid.

writes. But do we believe him? Grand occasions tend to bring out the worst in this working-class Northerner. The fanfare of farting brass he wrote in 1994 for the opening of the newly rebuilt Glyndebourne Opera House, summer retreat of the wealthy, is a case in point. (You might argue this was a rather futile gesture, given that he had already completed his first opera for the Glyndebourne stage, *The Second Mrs Kong*.) Why should he treat the Last Night of the Proms any differently? Part of me suspects a "plot" was hatched between Drummond and Birtwistle — two naughty schoolboys cocking a snook at an event where the Proms Season's musical priorities were downgraded in favour of a crass nationalism. We shall probably never know. What we can be certain of is that the critics, in writing about the work of this living composer in the way that they did, served to bring Birtwistle and his music to wide public attention. Ironically, every one of the critics — pro and anti — played his part in further canonising this composer.

ENCOUNTERING NEW MUSIC

This essay asks many more questions than it answers. I have inevitably only touched on a small handful of the problems that attend the activity of writing about the music of living composers, and how those of us who do this attempt to deal with those problems. Central among these problems is the figure of the composer, whose influence on what we do and say is often impossible to resist. Like the personal effects from Tracey Emin's life scattered about her bed, the words of composers are cast about the art they produce in such a way that we are happy to make connections between them, whether they exist or not. What is clear is that we need to be aware of the contexts within which we work, of the institutions that support and frame both the appearance of new work and the writing that accompanies it, of the cultural values we promote, and of our own roles and responsibilities in creating an appropriate climate within which new music can sympathetically be received.

Why do we continue to write about new music? It would be much safer to shut ourselves in an ancient library with some dusty manuscripts by a composer who has long since decomposed and who is in no position to answer back at any criticisms one might make. When writing about brand new music, we need to stick our necks out, we need to take risks. But that, surely, is the excitement of the activity? It still gives me a thrill to hear new works—in many sense, it is *only* new work that matters because it can tell us interesting, challenging, exciting or uncomfortable things about who we are now, it can help us see the world in which we live in new ways. I fully recognise that this is a rather utopian view of contemporary music as the vast majority of even classical music lovers want to have nothing to do with it (unless of course, like the current vogue for the music of John Tavener, it is music that comforts rather than confronts). But that—in part—is my job: to help people discover new music and enrich their lives in some way. A few years ago I made a CD for Glyndebourne which was an introduction to Birtwistle's opera *The Last Supper*, distributed free to anyone who wanted it. One old lady came up to me after a pre-opera talk I gave in Oxford and told me that she would not have come all the way from the Isle of Wight (a journey of *c.* 150 km plus a short sea crossing) to see the performance if my CD had not persuaded her that this was serious and powerful work worth taking seriously. "Joy shall be in heaven over one sinner that repents than over ninety-nine just persons, which need no repentance." (Luke XV: 16) It is a moment such as this that makes my work worthwhile.

THE GENESIS OF QUARTET NO. 4
Jonathan Harvey

Second only to my early years as a choirboy, the most important of my life have been my years as a quartet player — I played the cello. I played a great deal in public, but not professionally, though I was once asked to join a professional quartet. It was through my cellistic abilities that I met Irvine Arditti, when we both played in a small group which specialised in electronics with instruments, in the early 1970s.

He commissioned the Arditti Quartet's first commissioned quartet from me (Quartet No. 1, 1977). He and his colleagues have remained a model, unequalled and unique, for what is possible in this genre, and any account of how my new quartet was born must start with the enabling and inspiring force of that model, present throughout the thought-processes of my composing.

Three quartets later, in about 1996, we discussed the possibility of a fourth quartet, with live electronics. IRCAM was interested in commissioning it as part of an ongoing series with the Arditti Quartet. Gilbert Nouno, of IRCAM, and I had already resolved to work together on a new project: all these factors came together to cause the circumstances favourable to birth. In 2002 I would be able to work at IRCAM for a period of research, leading to a later period of realisation.

These are the outer circumstances; the inner ones were less cut-and-dried. Many of my recent works had played with a sort of alchemical distillation process. The sounds become less substantial, more delicate, closer to "spirit" or "emptiness" in the technical buddhist sense. My *Third Quartet* was one such example. It is perhaps a feature of string writing in our time that the possibilities of "noise" — *sul ponticello* and non-standard harmonics giving multiphonics for example — have seemed highly attractive. Lachenmann's quartets are a good example. At any rate, such was the thrust of my aesthetic in approaching the doors of IRCAM.

The Buddhist view of reality as lacking inherent existence from its own side is one of the most important insights into the "reality" of music that I know. With a deepened understanding of this view come a sense of impermanence, flux, insubstantiality, spaciousness and indeed tranquillity.

I have been very interested therefore in allowing the instability, the changeability, of music to be brought to the fore. With electronics this aspect would become even more striking, in my view. The possibilities of etherealising and refining the qualities of thought which are projected thematically by the quartet became enormous. For instance, the sound can be blurred, it can be changed seamlessly from one idea to another, from one timbre to another timbre. The sound can be made to fly spatially in a way that gives it a volatility, an ethereal quality. These were the main ideas that were in my mind when Gilbert Nouno and I started to play recordings of my earlier quartets and other quartets, such as Luigi Nono's *Fragmente—Stille, An Diotima*, into the various treatments and thus experimented on them. It was not an easy process, because the CDs that were being played into the computer had little or nothing to do with the sounds that would be played into the computer in the concert. So one had to imagine how such a treatment would affect often quite different sounds, which I was going to compose in the coming months.

The projection of the quartet into six or eight loudspeakers arranged around the hall meant that very tiny sounds could be amplified and used as musical substance. For instance, playing on the rib of the instrument, or on the tailpiece, or on the bridge without tone. When such indeterminate noise is treated with various pitch multiplications the effect is of musical shadows—of shadows being structuralised. Often the sounds are so soft it is almost as if silence itself is moving. And a continuous sound on the rib of the instrument is fodder for the spatialisation to construct a "metaphysical" rhythm, even a rhythmic thematicism. In Buddhist terms this struck me like the action of karma in one's life. All one's actions have consequences and they follow "like the shadow of a body", inseparably and invariably. Using electronics meant often that sounds the quartet played were recorded, stored in the computer, and then played back in transformed form later as a consequence of that earlier action. Karma is thought of as, ultimately, an illusion; so I thought of these shadowing sounds in the electronics as having a strong illusory quality to them, perhaps in contrast to the more substantial sounds which were conventional quartet music.

We worked with two spatialisers. A spatialiser is capable of projecting the sound around the hall and, by adding reverberation, even outside the hall to a great (and precise) distance. The mathematics of how the ear perceives distance and localisation are complex and have been the subject of research for several years at IRCAM.[1] The results now available to composers are superb. One can set up any number of loudspeakers, make a few adjustments to the parameters, which are quite simple, and the spatialiser will place the sounds in the various speakers so that no sense of the speakers themselves is present to the listener.

In order to make the spatialisation something more than just a cosmetic addition, I gave the rhythmic movements in space a thematic structure. The sounds would go from one part of the room to another, constantly changing position, going more or less through the centre — but not exactly, as that would give too much of a "bump". And this they would do at a certain speed of travel, either travelling rapidly at the beginning of the unit of time and then staying a little, or travelling throughout the unit of time and not staying at all (one could adjust all such parameters). It was also possible to rotate the sounds, and using a graphic pen on a circular tablet to lead the sound wherever the pen "wrote" on the circular tablet. This gave a truly gestural musicality to the diffusion performance.

Four rhythms were composed, each one consisting of about a dozen durations, and they were usually looped. The repetitive structural rhythm was by no means intolerable, in fact in the experiments forty or fifty repetitions of the loop as a counterpoint and background to the musical arguments of the quartet was completely acceptable, indeed very interesting; a polyphony of

---

1. Gilbert Nouno & Carlos Agon, *Contrôle de la spatialisation comme paramètre musical* (Paris: IRCAM Information File no. 22, 2002), pp. 95–99; Jean-Marc Jot & Olivier Warusfel, "Le Spatialisateur", in: *Actes du Colloque Le Son et l'Espace, Rencontres Musicales Pluridisciplinaires Informatique et Musique* (Lyon:. GRAME, 1995).

movement was set up which was completely absorbing. Of course, the tempo of the rhythms could accelerate or slow down and be transformed improvisationally by the graphic pen interfering at any point one wished. We had two graphic circles, in operation most of the time. One of these would be controlled by the pen and the other would be on automatic rhythmic looping.

Other types of treatment we experimented with were, first, harmonisation. There were several harmonisers set up, each capable of delivering five or six additional notes to the inputted note. Set to semitones, the resultant clustered sound was quite spectacular when mirroring changes of timbre like a transformation to *sul ponticello*. This was because the whole chord would change timbre in an extravagant and striking way. Quarter-tones on the other hand gave a more elemental, "less musical" effect more like nature; water and wind came to mind. This is the fascinating point at which music approaches close to nature, which is such an important topic in music of today and in a lot of my music too. The "natural" world displaces the "cultural" world of instruments. Eighth-tone clusters with the harmonisers sound almost like a big vibrato and have a chorusing effect, which again is quite distinctive from other musical purposes.

One of the most far-reaching treatments was that of granulation. This entails recording what the quartet play and either storing it as a buffer of a few seconds' duration or continuously rerecording the buffer so that after a little delay the treatment of what the quartet has just played will come out, like a following distorted echo. If a buffer is stored statically without renewal for a fair amount of time the granulator will read and cut the recording into tiny grains of sound (which can be shaped in any way one likes, to give different timbres and qualities) and these grains are read off the buffer at different points in the recorded few seconds of music. The reading-position can be fairly static, always in the same place, or can move along the stored sound slowly, so that very gradually the resultant sound colour changes as different pitches and timbres are addressed.

One can change the position of reading this stored passage in the buffer either quickly or slowly. In fact, one can make the position change by jumps with great volatility and mobility. This, of course, gives the opposite of the static, reverberatory quality of granulation as it is often thought of—something which is rather smooth and long. The quality here is of frenetic activity, a bit like Berio at his most active, or often in a rather delicate vein like Mendelssohn's fairy music, for example. These poetic qualities could be used on different quartet input to great effect, sometimes sinister and disturbing, sometimes light and dancing, and sometimes slow and mystical. All the transitions between them could be made by interpolation from one speed of mobility to another.

Again, the polyphony between untreated repeat of what the quartet is playing in ostinato looping form, and a frozen granulated buffer giving a quiet texture moving around the hall in different spatial rhythms is complex and exciting, and, of course, against this the live quartet will be adding yet a third layer.

I came to think of the frozen smooth sounds as having a spiritual quality and the more gritty, grainy, jumpy types of granulation to be materialistic. What would seem polyphony that is a little confused was immediately clarified by the separation of spatialisation—different types of movement across the hall characterising each layer.

Untreated recordings into the buffer of the quartet's sound are made on the fly with triggering. What happens after that could be determined in different ways. Either this recording loops unchanged, or new recordings are placed over it. If these new recordings are very short, perhaps only one per cent of the length of the original recording, then it would take at least a hundred new triggerings to obliterate completely the original recording, or probably many more. More normally short new recordings would gradually be added interspersed almost at random into the old recording, so bits of archaeological history, as it were, would gradually appear in the looped playback, which would continually change, updating itself partially, bit by bit, with new juxtapositions. One bit of time would be completely distant from another bit of time, with which it would be rubbing shoulders. Ultimately this depends on the type of music the quartet is playing, whether smooth and continuous or fragmented and changeable. The effects will of course be radically different. Quite often in the quartet I came to use two loop buffers of completely different recorded passages, of which one might be static and the other constantly updated.

Another important technique that we researched was vocoder time-stretch. If one uses a recorded buffer and loops it with an increasing stretch one can hear the passage become more and more reverberated, slowed down and stretched out. This can be combined with frequency shift, which changes the spectrum in a complex distortion, or with spectral inversion, which changes the amplitude of the partials from loud to soft and soft to loud. This latter gives a kind of ring modulation effect which reminded me of Stockhausen's *Telemusik*. That group of techniques was rather complex, and was probably best used with simple, melodic sorts of line. The two sides, left and right, could be stretched at different speeds making even more subtle the stretching out of the same material. It can become a little over-reverberant and "bathroomy" if the sound is too complex; nevertheless the effect is strange, even disturbing in that, unlike reverberation, actual motives are clearly audible coming through the wash of sound.

I came away from the research period at IRCAM with my head full of flying objects and shadowy sounds. As I mentioned above, many of my works have been concerned with an almost alchemical sublimation and etherealisation of material. For instance, *Mothers shall not Cry, Bird Concerto with Pianosong, Ritual Melodies* and the *Third Quartet*. Connected with this, an author I came upon in this subsequent period was the French philosopher and literary critic, Gaston Bachelard. He once marvellously wrote "aerial being is pure being." I was particularly taken with the book *L'air et les songes: essai sur l'imagination du mouvement*, and absorbed it avidly during the period before going back to IRCAM. He wrote:

> If we want really to know how delicate emotions develop, the first thing to do, in my opinion, is to determine the extent to which they make us lighter or heavier. Their positive or negative *vertical differential* is what best designates their effectiveness, their psychic destiny. This, then, will be my formulation of the first principle of ascensional imagination: *of all metaphors, metaphors of height, elevation, depth, sinking, and the fall are axiomatic metaphors par excellence*. Nothing explains them, and they explain everything. Put more simply, if a person is will-

ing to live them, feel them, and above all compare them, he realises that they have an essential quality and that they are more natural than all the others. They engage us more than visual metaphors do — more than any striking image can. And yet language is not particularly well-suited to them. Language, conditioned by forms, is not readily capable of making the dynamic images of height picturesque. Nevertheless these images have amazing power: they govern the dialectic of enthusiasm and anguish. Vertical valorisation is so essential, so sure — its superiority is so indisputable — that the mind cannot turn away from it once it has recognised its immediate and direct meaning. It is impossible to express moral values without reference to the vertical axis. When we better understand the importance of a physics of poetry and a physics of ethics, then we will be closer to the conviction that every valorisation is a verticalisation.[2]

Spatialised music seems to me the ideal bearer of this metaphor.

I returned to IRCAM to complete the work with the main poetic idea of writing a music which verges on silence. It turned out to be quite a long work, of some thirty-six minutes, which of course could not be completely concerned with near silence throughout. Nevertheless, there are five very significant lengthy passages of near silence. It fascinated me always to read of Richard Strauss's reaction to Debussy's *Pelléas et Mélisande*. He commented that he could not hear the music. One could understand exactly how music of such refinement and delicacy could have escaped the ears of Strauss, which is not to diminish him as a composer in any way; the difference between his ear and Debussy's is simply enormous. Therefore, if this new work was to be genuinely new, it had to hover on the edge of unreality, or rather on the edge of showing the world as delusion, will-o-the-wisp, "lightning in a summer cloud" or whatever quasi-buddhist image one likes to use: everything is changing, everything is evanescent. It is not really possible to make everything completely evanescent, though. Life is also

---

2. Gaston Bachelard, *Air and Dreams: An essay on the imagination of movement* (Dallas: Dallas Institute Publications, 1988), p. 11.

characterised by obsession — terrifyingly solid-seeming. The stronger the obsession the more mendacious it is likely to be. I conceived the form as five lives or five cycles in cyclic existence (the reincarnational structure of the Buddhist world view). These five movements are characterised by certain obsessions which are found in trace form in subsequent movements, as if the mental continuum that proceeds from life to life, connected to its karma, is making its presence felt. Incarnation is *caused* by obsession.

The first movement is tentative in its formal structure. It is born out of very shadowy sounds which move distinctly in space, but more like ghosts than embodied beings. Gradually figures begin to form themselves, interspersed with long pauses, and create a kind of "personality". Soon after, however, the disintegration of this personality begins, with granulation and perforation acting in downward transpositions, plunging the music gradually to ever deeper transpositions of the grains, with quite disturbingly huge bass sounds rushing through the hall at the end. There is an in-between period of darkness which repeats very closely the first opening section in its tentative disembodied effect; it is perhaps paradoxical that such perceptually wandering, loose structures are in fact a close repetition. The main difference this time is that they are treated with harmonisation, making the sound more complex and the harmonics, which come from non-standard fingering, more rich in content.

Up to this point I had little idea of the global form. I wanted to start, and follow wherever the material led me. Formal exigencies should emerge naturally from material. In general I do not like to foreclose their innate tendencies by means of form-plans. But now, at this point, I was able to foresee several (possibly five) cyclic movements resulting from what I had so far written. With each new day further and further distances began to come into view, as if one were climbing a mountain.

The second cycle became more confident, more rhythmically assured than the first and at the same time more thematically obsessive. Here advantage is taken of the electronic recording of live quartet sound and its ability to be looped; this is in itself an image of obsession — of repeating without much variation, without thought. All lives are characterised to some extent by obsession, by hobbyhorses, by mistakes which we go on making or illusions we go on clinging to, without ceasing.

From the material of the first cycle, and using four derived harmonic fields only, I invented a melodic chain consisting of six melodies which are interspersed by six combination melodies. The combination melodies add together the two melodies on either side to make a more complex structure: where one melody has a sustained note or a rest the other melody will insert some activity, and vice versa. This repertoire of twelve melodies leaves its tentative existence of the first cycle and becomes confidently promulgated in the second cycle as thematic working, with more than a suggestion of minimalist repetitiveness. Having attained quite a lengthy statement of its thematic content, the melody chain again, as in the first cycle, decays, disintegrates and gradually winds down. The recorded buffers characteristically have recordings of silence inserted into them. These recordings are of very small duration, so only gradually punch holes in the passage which was recorded in the buffer, causing its evaporation into particles and finally silence.

Again there follows a third "bardo" section, a passage which repeats the shadowy noises of the opening section but with yet another new type of treatment. This is the stretch technique described above, which is more complex than any before and pushes the music out into an other-worldly space even more strange (but with the same material) than in previous sections.

The third cycle which is now born is basically fairly slow; it is of a rather passionate and dark emotional quality, often using unison lines, which are constructed from one of the melodies from the previous cycle's melody chain, but in very slow motion. Other melodies from the melody chain are subsequently touched on — all with the echoing treatment of stretch, frequency shift and spectral inversion. The melodic obsessiveness eventually bursts into a rather skittish waltz passage, which seems to break out of the emotional darkness that has preceded it, and rise up to an almost hysterical accelerando and explosion. The treatments at this point are complex and consist of stretch, granulation and live buffer repetition; the latter is destroyed by the insidious insertion of silence. The whole texture crashes down and again ends in a death which is "silent" but coloured with breathing rhythms. These rhythms are also the rhythms of the spatialisation: distant for the empty lung, close-up for the full lung. The rhythms speed up, begin to take on life, but the whole in between section is now shorter than before, as if the continuing personality is becoming purer, less in need of "purification".

The fourth cycle is a rather simpler music, turning at times to pentatonic harmonies. There are brief memories and traces of earlier movements, but in general silence is much more pervasive, silence interrupted by very fleeting recordings and granulations from what has been played a few seconds earlier. The spatialisers become very energetic with this wispy material and make constant accelerandi and ritardandi as they fly around — often soft, in rapid and joyous movements. Nevertheless the effect is one of stasis; there's no climax; it is like a vibrating and alert meditational state. One might think of a monk's life or a life of spiritual aspiration.

Again there follows an in-between passage, but here it almost is too short to be closely related to previous such sections. From the fleeting airiness of cycle four, cycle five is born as a kind of melodic invention. The slow melody, which dominates it, is derived from a quick furtive tremolando melody which came right at the beginning of the first cycle. Here perhaps the most important feature in this gradually rising melodic structure is that the spatialisation is rotating at a stroboscopic speed, which makes it almost static. It's moving so fast that one has almost an impression of shimmer. As Bachelard said, (words which stuck in my mind at the time) there is "sumptuous radiance" or "profound heights". The lines of the four players twine around themselves, soaring ever higher to the end; and the whole is encased in this shimmering light, so to speak, which is the result of stroboscopic speeds of sound rotation, mostly around twenty-three times a second. The speed varies slightly to re-attain the sense of slow rotation, although, like the wheel in an early film, in fact the rotation is very fast, but the illusion is of slowly turning. The static dots seem to be everywhere, like an illuminated mist. Against this, the first violin has a more thematic line of cadenza-like freedom against the other players; this line is in rhythmic back-and-forth motion, which accelerates to an extraordinarily fast tempo so that it too seems to be static by the end, and subsequently it joins the rotational shimmer of the other instruments. A paradise garden with yellow wisteria and wooden bird sculptures was the dreamlike image. In Buddhist terms this would be called a "pure land".

PHILOSOPHY OF COMPOSITION
IS THERE SUCH A THING?

Helmut Lachenmann

My visit to the Orpheus Institute was, despite — or perhaps rather because of — intensive preliminary discussions with the organisers, ultimately not tied to any clearly-defined topic.

It is always exciting when a seminar on New Music has to choose its own title. Due to lack of time, however, and also with reference to a desirably timely encounter with the contribution from the philosopher Albrecht Wellmer — timely for the sake of enabling a dialogue within this time spent together — it seemed necessary at least to give my remarks a provisional title, one which I would later be able to elaborate upon in the course of discussion. I found for myself the following — admittedly somewhat long-winded — formulation:

On composition and the idea of retrieving the concept of art with reference to society, its "occidentally"-based restrictions, and not least the human need for self-realisation through the creative process.

The not entirely unpretentious notion of "retrieval" refers to the dictum pronounced by Karl Kraus, that tireless admonisher and prophet of the "Last Days of Man", which he recognised during the outbreak of the First World War in an ardent protest against the current political and national over-enthusiasm of a warmongering journalism; who in the 1930s, however, upon the Nazis' rise to power, abstained from further "burning" articles, whose futility and helplessness he realised, and saw only a single necessity: to "bring language to safety" in the face of such an all-suffocating barbarism.

This all-suffocating barbarism diagnosed by Kraus was not overcome through the two world wars — on the contrary, it came to infiltrate all areas of life in a fatally harmless guise: as a culture of "fun" whose universal, cheapened availability gives rise to a rapid devaluation of all that has been precious to us as artistic experience. We are thus today once again faced with the task of bringing art "to safety", even if the word "safety" may initially give us a start.

With reference to the "retrieval" of the concept of art postulated here, we should perhaps first shed a little more light on this obviously endangered notion, not least to distinguish it from its use in the context of non-European cultures. My — severely reductive — definition would be as follows: art — as it defines itself for us today within the European historical context — is a form of magic broken in and with spirit, broken in the name of a creative will that is increasingly realising its autonomous purpose, and accordingly reacting to the reality it constantly recognises anew. (Unquestionably, such a definition directly opposes the role afforded to art by society as a service-object — whether intensively or superficially employed — even in those contexts where it is granted an autonomous status.)

To the extent that the notion of an "autonomous will" has repeatedly become aware of its own questionable nature, the creative process has lost its innocence; it can no longer encounter the constraints it has to overcome in a naive fashion. Beauty — according to my own definition from twenty years ago — as the "denial of habit" (not of all things habitual!) — has, insofar as the term "habit" encompasses the idea of (...comfortably? thoughtlessly? safely? unemancipatedly?) "dwelling", the following meaning: an offer to break free from all security. It does, of course, thus assume the existence of aesthetic security, i.e. a naively intact bourgeois consciousness. The "retrieval of art" would thus — to expand upon Kraus' pronouncement — mean: bringing art to a place of in-security, discarding false securities, and doing this with reference to an innovatively-oriented work-ideal that subjects our experience of music to constant dialectical renewal.

My three theses on composing — which I here consciously present, not for the first time, as metaphors — are:

- Composing means: reflecting upon music
- Composing means: building an instrument
- Composing does not mean "letting oneself go", but rather "letting oneself come".

I have commented on these points at length elsewhere.[1] The first point relates to the demand for constant reflection, in the sense of searching, experimenting, sensitising oneself to the preformations of listening and of compositional resources, whether intellectually or intuitively controlled. This forms a part of the daily mental life of every creative spirit.

In this light, composing means an encounter[2] with composition *as such* and with its conditions. The latter entails both the en-*counter*, the breaking, and the mutual exposure to uncertainty, the personal risk and the responsibility towards society. Composing, after all, always takes place within an "administered", universally owned medium, in the form offered by tradition and public practice.

The second point concerns immediate creative practice, by which I mean the concrete process of composition, i.e. the temporally-articulated handling of sound-resources and/or sound-matter. Composers dabbling in philosophy, and finding themselves presumably out of their depth, can most readily make authentic statements in this context. This second point addresses the necessity of establishing a new system of categories in every work — naturally in dialogue with those already existing — and conceiving every work as a "syntactical blueprint". This aspect is to be the central focus of my investigations.

The third point concerns the role of intuition, the question of "freedom" of choice; it reminds us of the creative impulse as a liberated, "contented" phenomenon, i.e. one that does not suppress contradictions, but rather illuminates them, insofar as it exceeds what is rationally determinable.

The conditions of the material, whose need to be diagnosed and reflected upon is referred to in the first of my three propositions,

---

1. Helmut Lachenmann, "Über das Komponieren", in: *Musik als existenzielle Erfahrung* (Wiesbaden: Breitkopf & Härtel, 1996), p. 73 ff.
2. Translator's note: the German word *auseinandersetzen* has the meaning of engaging with or confronting something, and is here examined in its component parts: *auseinander* = apart, *setzen* = to place. Lachenmann extends the word-play by rearranging these particles to form *sich einander aussetzen*, meaning for two parties to expose themselves to one another, to drop their defences in the face of a possible mutual abrasion.

I would like to outline — again, not for the first time[3] — as follows:

— Every element subjected to compositional treatment is moulded in its material definition through our tradition, or at least stands in relation to it. Its requisites are: tonality with all its highly complex, polyvalent dialectics of consonance/dissonance, tonal/atonal, familiar/unfamiliar, homely/exotic, to name but a few areas of tension that constitute this aspect of its socio-historically based predisposition; also the traditional forms, tonal theories, as well as the accompanying musical practice in all its richness.

— Every element subjected to compositional treatment can be defined as an immediate bodily stimulus conveyed through physical information. All attempts to render this perceptible in the compositional act inevitably amount to a resistance against the aforementioned predispositions. This second condition dwells in the dialectic of the proposal of the "evident" through the withholding of that which has become convention. A glance at the physical, energetic, immediately perceptible anatomy of sound-events implies the exclusion of a mode of listening "polished" by tradition and habit. Nonetheless, a perceptual practice tied so directly to "acoustic data" is also ambivalent. For that which is experienced in all its physical immediacy for its part defines itself through, or perhaps represents, a context determined by the rules of play: itself open, at the same time, to being experienced as a structure, it reveals itself as a part, a message of a system, of a generative principle, as a component of a higher structure.

— The third condition is thus not in opposition to the second, as the second is to the first; it rather constitutes the upshot of the purely physical experience's unfolding. I define it as the structurality of sound as a newly individuated product of systems, rules, laws, temporally-articulated constellations.

— Finally, as the fourth condition, the "aura", i.e. the history of the material in wider, extramusical contexts, in all spheres of our social and cultural reality, of our conscious and subconscious awareness, our archetypal memory, both collective and individual.

---

3. Cf. Lachenmann, "Vier Grundbestimmungen des Musikhörens", in: op. cit., p. 54 ff.

The "aura" of each single sound, of the material, should not be confused with the aura of a work. I rather doubt, furthermore, that it is identical to what Albrecht Wellmer terms *Weltbezug*, i.e. relation to the world. It is difficult to establish, at any rate, whether or not this latter quality is contingent on the aura of each individual object. The notion of aura relevant here encompasses the necessary estrangement of locally auratic effects, alone through the necessity of losing its innocence in the realm of absolute sonicity and/or structural autonomy. (After all, what place does a cowbell — as atmospheric as it might sound — really have in the concert hall? ... One could equally think of the "horn-call" at the start of Beethoven's Piano Sonata op. 81a, *Les Adieux*, prefigured in a thousand symphonies of the Viennese School, and here given new expressive weight as a "farewell".)

Without a doubt, these four aspects not only encounter each other, they are even absorbed, even fall into one another (the "aura" of the tonal).

My four aspects are exemplified in Webern's op. 10 no. 4. Motivic shapes in the mandolin, trumpet, trombone, violin and viola form a constellation of melodic structures between the six notes of the opening mandolin figure and — in immediate succession — a single one (Bb" in the viola); they redefine one another in their timbral radiance through the melodic (= tonal) aspect which they at once invoke and disperse to the level of pointillism. Melody, reduced to a single point in the viola's entry on a harmonic, at the same time becomes the first link in a chain of increasingly irregularly perforated *tenuto*-gradations — such as the clarinet trill towards the end, or the regularly syncopated clarinet tenuto preceding it — before a radical dissolution in less and less evenly rhythmicised points, from the repeating closing figure in the mandolin, the irregular reiterations of harp harmonics, the strokes of the snare drum, the minor second played twice by the celesta, to the single harp sound at the start. The latter, as a dissonant = tonal triad, proves for its part the most opulent element in a constellation of impulses at whose opposite extreme stands the naked, dry, unpitched stroke of the snare drum. What I have here described as a structure, i.e. an overlaying of categorially-determined allocations, appears at once — in terms of its aura — as a "sérénade interrompue" "boiled down" to a few seconds: the mandolin motive, muted viola harmonic, muted trumpet- and horn-calls, clarinet syncopations/trills, irregular pulsations in the snare drum, the rhythms of harp harmonics and celesta, and the muted violin cantilena evoke an archetypal idyll within the most compressed of spaces: Mahlers *Nachtmusiken* from a bird's-eye view.[4]

One should note: what is here referred to as aura is intended as the aura of the resources invoked, and not that of the resulting work. For the work's aura can no more be questioned than verbalised, as little as can that of Beethoven's *Pastorale*, or Mozart's *Kleine Nachtmusik*, the latter equally a "serenade"…

The observation of the second aforementioned condition — that of corporeal or physical determination — may follow the sonic typology I "provisionally" conceived some 30 years ago, whose five forms — cadential sound, colour-sound, fluctuating sound, textural sound, structural sound, or indeed sound-cadence, tone colour, sound-fluctuation, sound-texture, sound-structure — derive successively from one another and — in part as sounds, in part as processes — dissolve the duality of sound and form, instead dialectically assigning the one to the other. The notion of "personal time" takes on a key role as the time required by the listener to recognise the physiognomy of an authentically-conceived sound or sound-vision; form, then, is in fact the "arpeggio" of a sound-space to be explored through listening. This does not overlook, it should be noted, the problem of equating the experience of a musical, and thus irreversible sequence with the exploration of a "space".

Schematically speaking, "structure" could thus be understood as a more or less complex projection and overlaying of allocations — though I sometimes prefer to term the latter "families": the separate projected particles take effect together, each in its own fashion, with regard to a common context as yet undergoing definition: each family member is an individual entity, not simply — as was the case in both the compositional and conceptual aspects of the original serial practice — quantitatively identifiable gradations

---

4. Cf. Lachenmann, "Hören ist wehrlos — ohne Hören", in: op. cit., pp. 121–123.

of a character already defined within each separate component. The overall profile of this family, after all, is not revealed simply through the "father" or the "youngest daughter"; at the same time, however, these are not mere fragments, but are rather each absolutely individual characters — at once autonomous and shaped by, as well as shaping for, the whole. The "total picture", as the overall experience comprising mutually relativising, i.e. specifying and intensifying sound-experiences, can scarcely be put into words; thus even the composer often does not know, cannot say exactly what he "intended", or perhaps what he "got himself into".

The concept of structure I have thus outlined at once fulfils and negates the "old" serial ethos. The systems on which the "families" are based no longer deal with naked, quasi-unconscious parameters, with quantifiable measurements and permutational mechanisms that know nothing of their own effects. In place of parameters we find "categories", one could also call them sound-"aspects", whose gradations are of a qualitative nature. These qualities can certainly be incommensurate, and the composer's decision to collect them as a "family" on the basis of a common core can mean that he must himself first discover what it is that connects them: under what roof can a trombone glissando and a harp pizzicato cohabit as members of one and the same family? We are, then, dealing with the secret of a uniting third party, a common denominator that often lies far beyond what can be acoustically measured. (In the context of string music, for example, the factor uniting the two sonorities — at an initially primitive level — would be their respective status as "foreign bodies"... The category of "foreign bodies" cold thus be presented in an unmistakable form, and perhaps the notion of a "foreign body" can even be developed and radicalised — perhaps to the point where what is posited as the "familiar" — in this case the strings — in fact transpires dialectically as the most profoundly foreign of all "foreign bodies"...)

Composing with reference to the structural sound perceives itself as an act of outlining, of positing, finding and inventing sound- or sound movement-related categories, and of developing a categorial system. To the extent that the notion of music as such thus reflects upon and redefines itself, this amounts to the development of syntactical blueprints. In the examples I have used so often from the works of Beethoven and Webern, one might add, such categories are themselves subjected to constant transformation: rather like a living being, which, while "living", at once ages, dies, and transforms itself, so that the idea of "living" is defined differently for a child, an adult (i.e. a former child), or an aged person, one for whom childhood lies in the distant past.

Compositional practice, as the implementation of categorial systems, the construction of sound-structures and structural sounds, will, with regard to those areas that are unknown and cryptic even to the composer, to that which he seeks and ultimately creates, be forced to approach the task from the wrong end time and time again. Technically speaking, the starting point for the act of composition — as it occurs at the work-desk — is almost always the quasi-serial/quasi-aleatory generation of a temporal grid and a complex of overlaid, but as yet nameless, purely fictitious "families" suspended within it. (Only rarely have I managed to derive the relevant information — number of family members, intervals between them, i.e. the overall rhythm of their projection — from the concrete sound-categories intended for application in a given work. This is simply because I have not usually understood them sufficiently myself, just as in earlier times a composer would perhaps not, upon writing down a motive, have known what transformations and wider implications would come to be associated with this motive. One cannot tell with every discarded stone whether and to what extent it might become a cornerstone.) In my case, such grids form the basis of works like *Kontrakadenz, Tanzsuite mit Deutschlandlied, Ausklang,* indeed also the opera *Das Mädchen mit den Schwefelhölzern.* (In the score version of my Second String Quartet that was on sale for a long time, I had added the work's temporal grid — the ametric pulse behind it, so to speak — above the score notation, and subsequently commented upon this procedure in my essay on the piece.)[5]

On occasions, I have even improvised such aperiodically pulsating "grids", for example the latent march-rhythm in its various augmentations and diminutions in *Fassade*; such improvisation, it

---

5. Lachenmann, op. cit., pp. 237–242.

should be noted, certainly obeys a "law" of its own — one that affects it internally, but without being distorted by a self-imposed bureaucratic rationale.

In *Tanzsuite mit Deutschlandlied* one also finds such dance-rhythms as waltz, valse lente, siciliano, gigue, polka, galopp, and songs like *Schlaf, Kindlein schlaf*,[6] or even the *Deutschlandlied*,[7] as grid-constituting formal skeletons. I referred to this mode of employing patterns as temporal markers in place of serially-generated rhythms as "reduced structures". The most striking examples of this can be found in *Fassade* (1972) and *Ein Kinderspiel* (1980), to the extent that the grid normally functioning covertly as a regulative system of temporal divisions between families and their members is now openly revealed as a sounding rhythm. The *Litanei* and *Epilog* sections of my opera also function in this manner.

To a certain extent, such patterns — as unfocused thoughts — belong to those explicitly stationary moments that dis- or interrupt the dynamically-conceived tendencies of my structures time and time again. In almost all of my compositions there is a moment of repose — in the manner of a fermata — in which the music glances around like a mountain-climber who only becomes aware of his new surroundings upon standing still, and only now experiences the characteristic stillness of the plateau he has reached. "Reduced structures" of this kind can be found equally in the works of such composers as Morton Feldman, in those of the more astute minimalists or of Cage, who preferred to leave it unreservedly at the bare generational processes. Other than with these composers, however, the dialectic of reception and repose in the terrain thus reached, thus conquered, thus crept up on, i.e. the overcoming of resistances forms, in my music, a vital part of the work-experience. Where the path is in fact the goal, I would rather not be brought to the summit of a mountain by helicopter; such quick service should be reserved for Sunday walkers.

The practice of generating temporal grids as initially empty vessels for a system of sounds that should unfold within it — and

---

6. Translator's note: a very popular traditional lullaby.
7. Translator's note: the German national anthem.

always also burst its seams!! — , which I have mentioned — albeit not described — here, is presumably an entirely personal way of getting a composition underway. It stands alongside equally productive, perhaps more assured and directed pre-compositional techniques used by other composers: one could think of Stockhausen's *Gruppen, Mantra*, his method of formula-composition in general, or of his interesting — stillborn — *PLUS-MINUS*; of permutational ceremonies such as in Boulez' *Rituel*, or of the temporal divisions employed by Ferneyhough.

It seems necessary to me to reflect upon that which is located behind the label of "categories". In order to escape from the mannerism of tone-colour heroes on the one hand, and the neo-surrealism inherent in orgies of defamiliarisation on the other, as well as the prison of pointillist thought — not least also to avoid degrading sound to mere objective information, as it were to a formal building-block, instead allowing it to become a genuine event — I have developed, since *temA* (1968), an approach revolving around what I have termed "musique concrète instrumentale". Sound as something real and palpable, as a "natural phenomenon" taking place here and now, evokes a mode of listening previously excluded from the musical medium, or at least neglected in reflections upon it, which treats sound — be it natural or artificial, given or constructed — as a phenomenon of nature. The titles of my works *temA, Air, Pression, Dal niente, Guero, Kontrakadenz, Klangschatten — mein Saitenspiel*, later also *Ausklang* and *Harmonica*, all try to point to the ambivalence between the "work" and corporeal sound-experience. One can urgently sense how this aspect, novel if at all only for being pushed into the centre of compositional thought, is hinted at in a consciously controlled form in pre-Baroque music; it can be ascertained in the music of the Mannheim and Viennese Schools as an apparently superficial specification serving to simplify formal structure, more strongly — for breaking out of standardisation — in the works of Beethoven and Schubert; more clearly in Bruckner's works than Brahms', more in Mahler's than in Strauss', more in Debussy's than in Ravel's, more in Varèse's than in Ives', more in Berg's *Wozzeck* than in *Lulu*, more in Webern's pre-dodecaphonic works than Schönberg's; in serialism we occasionally find it sabotaging the clarity of the abstractly-conceived hierarchy of categories. It is present in a frequently surrealistic, and thus harmless form in the works of Ligeti and Kagel, more strongly in *Apparitions* than in *Atmosphères*, and evident as something consciously brought to the light of examination in my own works of the late 1960s, for example *temA, Notturno, Pression, Air*, or *Kontrakadenz*.[8]

With all works thus oriented I realised, however, that the procedural stringency must go beyond the immediate experience of "palpability", however it may have been developed, if it is not to lose its way in the botanical or the playful: at the edges of this compositional approach there appeared such previously excluded, old — though in this context rejuvenated — categories of sensation as rhythm, consonance, melody, pathos, which must be uprooted from their bourgeois commodification and invoked in all their "dangerousness". They are "dangerous" for resisting every form of domestication, only thus corroding the boundaries of the old, ruling idea of music and sabotaging its etiquette.

Any attempt to illustrate the play of categories by means of examples is in danger of contributing to the reification of such structural thinking. Nonetheless, I shall risk an example: in the central section of my piece ...*zwei Gefühle*... the guitar, or rather its "naked", stereotypical, "artless" combination of fourths, i.e. E minor with A and D, takes on a key role as a signal of a "nature-loving", as it were "open air" sound. It thus proves a member of a family of "pseudo-guitars" all identifiable through the same, albeit transposed, intervallic structure: piano, harp, timpani and six-part brass chords join in with the playing on open guitar strings — now faithfully transposed, now intentionally "detuned", or, in the case of the timpani, reduced to a collection of fourths produced by only four bodies of resonance; the guitar itself becomes, via the displacement of its "natural sound" through bar-chords, a "pseudo-pseudo-guitar". The aspect of artlessly stimulated open strings involved here allows, however, the inclusion of all other open strings: not only those of the multiply-retuned violin family,

---

8. Cf. my work-descriptions in various parts of *Musik als existenzielle Erfahrung*, op. cit., in particular in the essay "Hören ist wehrlos — ohne Hören", esp. pp. 124–6.

with their most elementary of natural harmonics, but also those of such strange stringed instruments as the piano and the harp, where, after all, open strings are played on exclusively. Through this immanently anticipated act of opening, the category initially taken as a basis is transformed to such a degree that even the low D flat that introduces the following section proves to be a virtual "guitar" sound. Perhaps this is an appreciable example of the dialectical alteration of a sound without any procedures of defamiliarisation: through the change of context, the low piano D flat is redefined as a further pseudo-guitar sound.

The role of instrumental defamiliarisation can only be touched on here. Formerly a somewhat grotesque element of pseudo-radicality in post-serial works that regressed to neo-surrealist or expressionist posturing—and for this reason one which such composers as Stockhausen, Boulez or Nono, not without reason, avoided with suspicion—, such distortions became, in the context of my notion of a "musique concrète instrumentale", an almost everyday part of my reservoir of energetically-determined or -controlled, graded sound-families. In *Notturno* (1966), *temA* (1968), *Pression* and *Air* (1969), and *Kontrakadenz* (1970) they allowed for a re-positioning of the aural antenna, equally in *Gran Torso* (1971) and *Klangschatten—mein Saitenspiel* (1972). But in the last of these they had already congealed, as it were, and were as such almost consciously standardised; they became the retrievable apparatus of an admittedly expanded, yet ultimately self-contained sound-culture of an almost classicist standard that could "happily" dispense with further pseudo-radical, botanical explorations, as the wealth of new sounds had not been discovered as an end unto themselves, but rather for the sake of sensitising our listening capacity in new ways. Certainly, there are always new instrumental techniques to discover; there is no need to avoid them. But "new sounds" as such are not the point; rather a mode of listening that constantly renews itself through reflection, and which must show equal proficiency in dealing with familiar and unfamiliar sounds alike—though the latter seems rather more easily achieved, in the sense that it bypasses genuinely innovative claims, instead withering away in the sonically "interesting"—i.e. boring—no man's land of exotic defamiliarisatory acrobatics.

What has been described here by no means concludes our examination of categorial notions. During the compositional process, anyhow, there constantly transpire — in the best case — new perceptual levels that can be defined categorially, and subsequently guided and controlled — and which at the same time open our imagination and our visions to unsuspected discoveries. In addition to this, however — and this should on no account be overlooked — we find categorial systems time and time again in differently conceived compositional methods which do, perhaps, treat the work as a sort of informational mechanism or organism, but expressly with reference to a process of reception that extends beyond mere structuralist virtuosity to the point of transcendence. I would consider Boulez the point of reference for this variety of musical thought. In the works of such composers as Elliott Carter or Brian Ferneyhough — to name two creative forces far removed from one another — , this model is by no means copied; but their dominant technical criteria are closer to the old serial parameters, and can accordingly be quantitatively examined and developed more easily. They can more readily be attributed to the Webern of the *Symphony* op. 21, with its rigid, but also self-assured constructive regulations, than to the early orchestral pieces, whose spirit influenced works such as mine or those of N.A. Huber. Their forms are more abstract, often more complex, and they are often constrained to pay for this complex, perhaps algorithmically-generated context the price of a restricted sonic panorama, where precisely that which is quantifiable is developed and permuted, sometimes allowing virtuosist or expressionist elements to re-enter through the back door of "écriture". Nonetheless, the results — depending on how complexity and creative intelligence meet for true structuralist adventures — can indeed be no less exciting, in sonic terms frequently even more mysterious, than those which take sound-invention and aspects of immediate sonic corporality as their point of departure.

What seems central to me as an object of compositionally-motivated "reflection upon music" is: the "world-relation" (*Weltbezug*) — to use Wellmer's term — of that which is seized upon by the categories placed into a work by the composer. "World-relation", it seems to me, bypasses what we think of as "social reality", and comes down to whatever kind of compositionally-evoked archetypes we experience ourselves in, beyond or perhaps within our definitions in socialised contexts as — clearly privileged — creatures which, presumably capable and desirous of gaining insight, "freeze in the sensation of uncertainty for a while" when experiencing music. If and how — to allude to Lukács' *Aesthetics* — the "whole human" is to recognise himself and his purpose in the "human as a whole" — this is where such an investigation should be taken up.

The debate on this aspect has yet to take place; its theme would have to be "structure and world-relation". At the same time, however, I recoil here and break off: woe to us if we reach "statements" through questions. Whatever composers cannot speak of they should work on. Work-analyses should, at least, perceive their own role as material descriptions as exceeding a mere reflection upon "categorial" issues and their associated systems, should remind themselves "silently" that, at the heart of what they deal with, there always lies "world".

In attempting such overtures — as informative as they may be, and as much as they might sensitise us to this aspect —, something will always be lost en route. From my seminars at the Orpheus Institute I would mention — and at the same time revoke — such examples as the following: the first movement of Beethoven's *Moonlight* Sonata as a hybrid of archetypes such as funeral march and serenade, the repeating triplets of the opening theme of the *Jupiter* Symphony as the estranged roll on a snare drum, recalling the military representational posturing of a feudally-governed society and — turning the tables — in the funeral march of the *Eroica* not only slowed down to the point of desolation, but indeed brutally dismembered and even turned back upon itself. Such matters are more related to what I have above termed "aura", and hardly touch upon the quality that "world-relation" should imply, if this latter is to guarantee a work's relevance and stringency. "World-relation": not something which any interpretational gymnastics will bring us closer to.

But to be "lost en route" does, at least, imply seeing a way, keeping a goal in view, not least in an age that reacts to its lack of orientation with coquetry and ostentation.

Philosophy of Composition?

Perhaps there is no need for so many new words: "How the spirit rules over everything…!", Nono once wrote to me.

"Yes — whatever is to touch the heart must come from above. Otherwise it is the more stuff of notes, a body without a soul." This was how Beethoven formulated it.

This only leaves the question: where is "above"…?

ON MUSIC AND LANGUAGE[1]
Albrecht Wellmer

I.

I would like to begin with a question: is there a language of music? Is music "speech-like" (*"sprachähnlich"*)? A strange question, for it is initially unclear what is even being asked. And if we were at least able to give the question a clear sense, could there then be a *general* answer? One has, for example, spoken of an end of speech-likeness in music in the context of the developments in the 20th century, in particular the abandonment of "tonality" and the development of serial techniques, or perhaps more generally a "parametric" mode of thinking, in New Music, as well as new forms of "concrete" or electro-acoustic sound-production; this state of affairs was interpreted either as a liberation or a loss. And if there were indeed such a thing as the end of speech-like music, how could it be read as an expression of a historical change in music — not one affecting only music or even all the arts, but rather the dawn of a new socio-historical epoch? These are questions to which no answer can be expected as long as the sense of our opening question — "Is there a language of music?" — is still unclear. Is it the question of whether music "says" or "expresses" something which could not be said or expressed in any other way, or the question of whether music has a "content", that is a reference to something extra-musical, or is it rather the question of whether music is a system of signs comparable to that of verbal language, as some semioticians claim, or whether it contains a

---

1. This paper for a seminar over several days at the Orpheus Institute in Ghent contains parts of the following previously written texts: "Das musikalische Kunstwerk", in: Andrea Kern & Ruth Sonderegger (ed.), *Falsche Gegensätze*, Frankfurt a. M. 2002; "Sprache — (Neue) Musik — Kommunikation", in: Gianmario Borio (ed.), *L'orizzonte filosofico del comporre nel ventesimo secolo*, Bologna 2003; "Über Negativität und Autonomie als ästhetische Kategorien: Hat die Musik etwas mit Wahrheit zu tun?", lecture held at the Lachenmann symposium during the Salzburger Festspiele 2002 (unpublished).

"syntax" or "grammar" in a similar manner to verbal language? What all these questions implicitly ask is what it is that makes (or can make) music so meaningful and important, not only for composing or performing musicians, but also for the music's *listeners*. Naturally this question must be posed for all the arts, but its need arises more urgently in the case of music than in literature, the visual arts or film: for their "world-relation", and thus also their potential existential significance, was never in question. Even in abstract painting, or with some forms of advanced poetry, where this world-relation could perhaps seem doubtful, it is nevertheless, I believe, no coincidence that a clearly palpable, an obvious world-relation in most examples of literature and visual art until now can hardly be disputed.[2] Music, on the other hand, is abstract by its very acoustic material; one could perhaps say — in reference to Nietzsche — that, through the long-standing connection between music and poetry in the development of tonal music, "the musical form was entirely enwoven with conceptual and emotional threads"[3] — which was the essence of its expressivity and semantic significance (that is, speech-likeness) —, but does one not also find — since serial music at the latest — an emancipation of music from such "conceptual and emotional threads" towards the materiality of the pure sound and its structural organisation, that is towards a retreat from "linguality" and from extra-musical reference? And could one not moreover say that only through this retreat can music truly become an "absolute" art form, one that is free from the yoke of extra-musical purposes and intentions and need obey only its own rules? I shall go on to refute this claim shortly, but for the moment the question shall remain unanswered.

This question is, in fact, not a new one. Eduard Hanslick, an important musical theorist of the 19th century, made — in a polemic against what he termed the aesthetic of "putrid emotionality", and in defence of an absolute, pure and autonomous instru-

---

2. As far as the visual arts are concerned, the Documenta XI in Kassel in 2002 offered particularly powerful examples of this.
3. Friedrich Nietzsche, *Menschliches, Allzumenschliches*, in: *Werke* vol. 1 (ed. by K. Schlechta), Munich 1960, p. 573.

mental music — the claim that "forms transported in sound are the one and only content and object of music."[4] This hypothesis constituted not only a stance in the disputes among musical theorists in the 19th century, but was also to gain a direct relevance in the quarrel on musical programmatics between Brahmsians and Wagnerians. In a slightly different context — namely with reference to the situation of post-tonal music — we find an updated version of this dispute in Dieter Schnebel's *Der Ton macht die Musik: Wider die Versprachlichung*, a polemical text written in 1990, where he criticises Adorno's notion of "speech-likeness" in music. Before I now return to my opening question I would like to take a brief look at Schnebel's critique, for it clarifies one particular point that is to be of importance in the following discussion. Adorno had advanced the theory — in opposition to early serialist tendencies — that without an element of speech-likeness, in other words: without a relation to the non-musical domain, music could only decay into a senseless kaleidoscope of sounds; he was guided in this assumption by his experience of the important directions in European music, from Monteverdi to the atonal phase of the Second Viennese School. Arguing against Adorno's idea of "speech-likeness" in music and his concern as to its loss in serial music, Schnebel draws attention to the productive aspects of this tendency towards a "delingualisation" of music in the serial and post-serial music of the 20th century.[5] According to Schnebel, Adorno's postulation of the constitutive speech-likeness of music is indeed in keeping with the tendency towards an increasing lingualisation of music in the 19th century, especially since Beethoven, and culminating in the musical "prose" of free atonality in the Second Viennese School; with the development of the twelve-note technique, however, and then increasingly in serial and post-serial music, a productive counter-movement "away from language" began. What Schnebel wishes to show is that the free atonal prose of works like the monodrama *Erwartung* is in reality an expression of a dilemma: the dilemma that, once the formative potential of

---

4. Eduard Hanslick, *Vom Musikalisch-Schönen*, Darmstadt 1991, p. 32.
5. Dieter Schnebel, "Der Ton macht die Musik oder: Wider die Versprachlichung", in: *Anschläge — Ausschläge. Texte zur Neuen Musik*, Munich 1993.

tonal music was no longer available, music temporarily lacked the means of forming independent, genuinely musical structures; composers were hence forced to rely on literary texts as an expressive basis. Schnebel thus sees in the "speech-likeness" of atonal music prior to the discovery of the twelve-note technique above all a lack of genuinely *musical* structural formation, which he addresses in order to point out the important difference between a genuinely *musical* context and a lingually-articulated semantic context. According to Schnebel, neither the material of music nor the central methods of creating musical forms and contexts can be understood in terms of the analogy to lingually-articulated semantic contexts: for him, musical form is rather the configuration of an acoustic, sounding material for which categories such as repetition and variation, periodicity and irregularity — that is, a formative play of identity and difference — are constitutive, not any speech-like aspects. While, for Adorno, the possibility of a musical sense and a musical context depends on the speech-like aspects of music, Schnebel sees in the "lingualisation" of music a danger of *diluting* the musical context. The slogan "away from language" can thus be viewed as a return to the genuine — in relation to the acoustic material of music — methods of constructing musical contextuality.

I would like to use Adorno's concept of music's speech-likeness and the counter-argument formulated by Schnebel as an opportunity to reflect anew upon the complex relationships between music and language, relationships that are not so much elucidated as obscured by Schnebel's apparently clear opposition of thesis and antithesis. In attempting first of all to distinguish between different ways in which one can speak of an internal *connection* between music and language, I intend to show at the same time that the alternative formulated by Schnebel, as suggestive as it may seem at first glance, is ultimately a false one. Only by going beyond this alternative shall it be possible to understand correctly both Adorno's claim of a necessary speech-likeness of music and Schnebel's insistence on its alinguality, and upon the necessarily "formal" means of creating a musical context; only then shall it be possible to determine whether, or indeed in what sense, the music of the 20th century has tended towards a move "away" from language, or what changes—if any—the relationship between music and language underwent in the 20th century. I shall therefore avoid directly addressing the question raised by Schnebel; I would prefer initially to clarify the polyvalence of the lingual topos in its application to music—Ferneyhough speaks of a "minefield of music/language analogies"—in order to subsequently reformulate the question as to how close to and/or how remote from language music actually is.

II.

One can examine the internal relationship between music and language from at least five different perspectives. I shall discuss four of these, relating to possible dimensions of speech-*likeness* in music, in this first part of my investigations. The fifth aspect of the relationship between music and language, which pertains to the constitutive speech-*relation* of music and its implications, shall be addressed following this.

1. One relationship between music and language was absolutised in the Romantic topos of music as the language of emotions (or affects), which played a central part in the music-theoretical discussions from Rousseau to Wagner, particularly also in early German Romanticism. This topos can most easily become comprehensible by—in Rousseau's and Wagner's sense—understanding music as something "split off" from an originary language in which the sonic, expressive and gestural aspects of language had not yet been separated from the conceptual aspects. (The human voice, with its phonetic and expressive possibilities, bound to a body that gesturally accompanies its speech/song.) Here, then, music is presented as an art whose roots lie in the phonetic-expressive, dynamic and gestural aspects of lingual communication. Music and communicative (i.e. discursive, conceptual) language are both attributed, one could also say, to a common lingual origin; and, just as emotions can be expressed and conveyed without words in the "musical" dimension of speech, music—according to this topos—takes on and refines this "a-conceptual" dimension

of lingual communication, as it were, on its path to a separation of the phonetic-expressive function from a verbal language being increasingly reduced to its conceptual dimension. Hegel still had something similar in mind when he wrote that in music, "the sphere of subjective inwardness" attains its consummation in tones: "Here, music spreads out into an expression of all particular emotions, and all nuances of good humour, gaiety, jesting, moodiness, rejoicing and cheering of the soul, equally the gradations of fear, worry, sadness, lament, anguish, pain, yearning etc. come to form the remarkable sphere of musical expression."[6] Music as the language of emotions is a language for the reason that it takes up the possibility already contained in the phonetic, rhythmic and gestural characters of everyday speech for a-conceptual utterance and the expression of feelings and affects, and at the same time — as an art form — infinitely expands the possibilities of the "natural" language of emotions.

2. A second aspect of the relationship between music and language — an aspect that can hardly be distinguished clearly from the first I have named, which rather transposes it into a new context — is given in the "world-relation" of music. One could also speak of a "representational aspect" of music, as became apparent, for example, in the musical rhetoric of the pre-classical era, and later — in a different fashion — in the forays into programme music in the 19th century. One could list countless examples — from Monteverdi and Bach to Messiaen, Kurtág and Lachenmann — in which the music, as it were, directs our attention towards something outside itself, evokes it, "represents" it, presents it in a new light or simply transforms it into music. This is not simply a matter of depicting passions and sensations, anger, pain and sorrow, as in opera since the time of Monteverdi; the issue is rather a musical representation or evocation of dramatic intensifications, of nature's fury or serenity, of struggle and farewell. To a certain extent, the insertion of extra-musical correlates in music can surely be explained by the synaesthetic character of everyday experience:

---

6. Georg Wilhelm Friedrich Hegel, *Vorlesungen über die Ästhetik III (Werke* vol. 15), Frankfurt a. M. 1970, p. 150.

I am involved in every perceptual act with my body, a multi-sensually receptive and active body, and this means that a relation to the other senses, and thus a latent world-relation, is always attached to the acoustic material of music. This explains, for example, the possibilities of "tone painting" in music: storms, gales, magical fires, forest murmurs, the play of the waves. As a rule, however, expressive and illustrative aspects will always be entwined from the outset, just as our experience of nature is always already "attuned" to us, is affectively or existentially relevant to our lives. For this reason, "images" of nature can also become means of evoking affective and existential sensibilities, as the example of Schubert's *Winterreise* amply demonstrates: in the images of barren winter wastes, ice, winter storms, of frozen tears and of death we find an increasingly condensed expression of fatal sorrow, an expression of the forlorn existence of the homeless wanderer exiled from his world. This example certainly shows that the question of world-relation in music cannot simply apply to extra-musical "references", in the sense of expressive contents and "tone painting"; at the same time — and more importantly still — it is rather a matter of a "world-relationship", as Adorno in particular showed repeatedly in his major musical analyses, precisely with regard to instrumental works — from Beethoven to Mahler, Schönberg and Webern.

Naturally, the question remains as to how something like this can be possible in purely instrumental music; the examples that immediately come to mind are those where music and language join forces, as in song or opera, and where the world-relation is thus automatically predefined according to the text or the dramatic action. A further example: Mozart's *opera buffa* works, in which — as Ivan Nagel has shown — a new human type and a new relationship of these humans to one another becomes apparent: the type of the autonomous bourgeois subject, which has now broken free from the bonds of feudal subjugation and appears in the Mozartian ensembles as a belligerently companionable society of the equal and the free. I would like to cite a few sentences by Nagel: "The ensemble, most untotalitarian of totalities, is the emblem of Mozart's *buffe*. One cannot decide whether its worlds are utopias, or otherwise... it is almost the only non-utopian, presentially unyearning topos which the newer arts have spawned. This means: its fulfilment is already there before it approaches with the end. It lives in the gift of all people to communicate unreservedly: as the luminous, complete presence of every individual in the relationship he initiates with all others, be they friend or foe. 'Fulfilment' only ultimately means that one's wishes or hopes will come true... first and foremost, it means that everyone lives together with everyone else in love and struggle (and only thus... truly learns to wish and hope.)"[7] This is no image of an existing society, but neither is it a utopia — in so far as utopias are something beyond the finite sociality of mankind, something beyond the conditions of love and death. It is an image of *human* happiness, as perhaps only music — and only in exceptional historical circumstances — can convey it. After Mozart, above all during the age of Restoration following the French Revolution, such music was no longer possible.

Our question was: does purely instrumental music have a world-relation, a connection to the extra-musical domain, can a world-relationship be articulated also in this medium? Our own world-relation and world-relationship, and equally our relationship to ourselves, are initially only possible in and through language; world-relation and world-relationship both assume the existence of language. But *what* and *how* is language? We initially tend to associate verbal or discursive language with this term; I would argue, however, that any understanding of language would be insufficient which failed to encompass alongside verbal language also the roots of musical, visual or choreographic forms of expression and representation. The different media are connected *in* language; even if each has its own irreducible possibilities of shaping and expression, each latently incorporates the presence of all the others, not least of verbal language, which can for its part be characterised in terms of a latent intermediality. It is due to the latent intermediality of music — as the other side of its world-relation — that even "absolute" music is automatically always bound up in a

---

7. Ivan Nagel, *Autonomie und Gnade. Über Mozarts Opern.* Kassel 1991, p. 36.

potential relationship of reciprocal correspondences, ruptures, illuminations and complementarities to the other artistic media, but particularly verbal language. This latter takes on an exceptional status to the extent that it is the medium in which we interpret and criticise art, in which we can argue about the quality of works of art and in which we attempt to clarify what and how art is. The intermediality of all artistic media, i.e. their common share in language, is in fact also what explains the possibilities of unifying these media to form "intermedial" aesthetic configurations in the first place, where the relationship between the individual media can be conceived as one of mutual interpretation, complementarity, inspiration or also subversion. It is almost as if every aesthetic configuration bound to a particular medium contained a cavity, as it were a layer of meaning which can no longer be articulated within this medium, which can only be brought to light and subsequently articulated through the addition of another medium. What is simultaneously inherent in the possibility of unifying different artistic media, however, is the possibility of their reciprocally affecting one another. Using Wagner as an example, Adorno pointed to the musical innovations which can result from binding music to the extra-musical parameters of drama; Wagner himself had already defended Liszt's programme music in the same sense. Conversely, referring to the symphonies of the Viennese School, Georgiades emphasised the development of those musico-linguistic elements without which the complex dramatic contexts of Mozart's operas would have been impossible. He refers to such aspects as discontinuity, contrast, unforeseen action, or sudden change in the formal structure developed above all by Haydn, where the unforeseeable quality of certain situations is articulated musically. "Without it [this structure], Mozart's musical theatre would have been inconceivable."[8] To name a final example, Adorno also pointed out that some of Schönberg's most important harmonic discoveries can be attributed to the singularities of Art Nouveau poetry, such as Dehmel's *Erwartung*. And not only this: it is precisely with reference to Schönberg's *Erwartung*

---

8. Thrasybulos Georgiades, *Musik und Sprache*, Berlin/Heidelberg/New York 1984, p. 95.

that Adorno speaks of the musically formative potency of the literary source: "The conflicts between physical urges, whose sexual origin Schönberg's music leaves no doubt about, have taken on a force in this protocol-like music that forbids any comforting placation. The protagonist of the monodrama *Erwartung* is a woman searching for her beloved at night, exposed to all the horrors of the dark, only to find him murdered at the end. She is turned over to the music, so to speak, as a patient of psychoanalysis. It forces her into a confession of hatred and desire, jealousy and forgiveness, revealing, beyond these, the entire symbolism of the unconscious; and the music recalls its right to offering comfort only once the heroine has lost her mind. The seismographic documentation of traumatic shocks, however, simultaneously becomes the technical determinant of the musical form. It precludes continuity or development. The musical language is polarised to its extremes: gestures of shock, almost physical convulsions, and the glassy stillness of one frozen with fear. It is this polarisation that the entire formal world of the mature Schönberg, and equally that of Webern, depends on. It destroys the musical "mediation" which their school had previously taken to an unprecedented level — the difference between theme and development, the constancy of the harmonic flow, the unbroken melodic line. One can gain insight from this into the entwinement of form and content in all music. All forms of music, not only since Expressionism, are precipitations of content."[9]

Adorno describes the musical form of *Erwartung* as being defined by the shocks of the panic-stricken course of the "plot" supplied by the literary source, through which the music is imbued with various entirely new contents naturally related to the destruction of the traditional conceptions of the subject in the age of psychoanalysis. In the music's structure we find the reflection of a decentred subject, as later enforced by the post-modern critique of the traditional notion of the unified, self-transparent and self-deter-

---

9. Theodor W. Adorno, *Philosophie der neuen Musik* (*Gesammelte Schriften* vol.12), Frankfurt a. M. 1975, p. 47.

mined bourgeois subject—and thus also a crisis in modernity's self-identity. In peculiar contrast to Schnebel, Adorno therefore views musical form as something that is not independent from the "content", that is the world-relation of the music. It is this opposition (between the perspectives of Adorno and Schnebel) that shall continue to occupy us later on.

As I have already argued, the relationship between the various media can be one of reciprocal correspondence or intensification, or equally one of rupture, re-illumination or subversion. An example of the latter could be seen in Mozart's Requiem. Some time ago, I attended a performance of the Requiem at a church in Berlin—framed and repeatedly interrupted by Henry Purcell's *Funeral Music for Queen Mary*—, a performance with an additional commentary in the form of text interludes spoken by Walter Jens. It became clear to me upon this occasion to what extent Mozart's music acts subversively towards the clerico-theocratical, authoritarian and apocalyptically threatening dimensions of the liturgical Requiem text. On several occasions, Mozart transforms the terror of the *Dies Irae* into a collective singing that overcomes mere terror, where an ounce of *human* reconciliation, solidarity, an *atheistic* faith shines forth—perhaps in a similar sense to that intended by Bloch when he spoke of "atheism in Christianity". Jens referred to this as the dimension of a *Magic Flute*-like reconciliation in Mozart's Requiem. It is by no means here a matter of beautifying the reality of death—rather of giving the "Death, where is thy sting / Hell, where is thy victory"-motive the most plausible turn that is humanly possible. In this context, Jens also mentioned the anecdote in which, only a few hours before his death, Mozart gathered various friends and relatives around his bed to sing (Mozart taking the alto part) parts of the Requiem with them (was it the *Lacrimosa*?), and suddenly burst into tears. The performance of the Requiem did indeed end with the *Lacrimosa* (thus omitting those parts which had been newly composed by Süßmayr), so, at the end, the choir sang the eight bars of the *Lacrimosa* which Mozart himself had managed to complete—thus breaking off after the first major climax. And then only a final rendition of Purcell's funeral march.

This reciprocal influence of the various art-media on one another may, to stay on the subject of music, occur in both directions: extra-musical impulses can force composers to effect musico-linguistic innovations, and musical innovations may offer the first chance to access new "semantic fields"—in music-drama or in song, for example. To put it another way: with respect to a given extra-musical field of meanings the music can open a dimension through which this field of meanings appears in an entirely new light, and seems charged with new complexity; conversely, extra-musical semantic and experiential content can trigger off an intra-musical development of the musical material. Neither aspect comes first in this constellation: extra-musical meaning and musical material are to equal degrees determinants and results of a complex process, in which the media of the various arts develop in part according to their own logic, in part according to the logic of reciprocal inspiration, reciprocal correspondences and also reciprocal subversion. In this manner, by means of intra-musical development, equally through connecting music to other media of art —dance, poetry, drama and even the visual media—, music's world-relation as evident through the history of European music was brought to light in the most different of directions, and at the same time the world was made audible in ever new ways as a historical and a natural space.

Yet it is precisely because the world-relation of the arts refers back to language and dimensions of linguality that it cannot be grasped through a semiotics of the arts: the arts do not develop any as it were self-sufficient sign-systems of their own, but can rather be grasped in their semantic content and their significance only on the basis of their complex relation to verbal language. An additional reason, however, for which a semiotics of the arts can only fail, is—to stay on the subject of music—that the world- and language-relation presented thus far does not yet reveal anything about music as an *art* form. In order to speak of music as an art, we must not only take into account that the acoustic material of music is for the most part not natural, that it is rather one which has been brought forth historically, which has been produced for the most part with technical means, and which undergoes historical change; we should rather take up Schnebel's question and ask how a specifically musical, that is an *aesthetic context* can be brought forth with the aid of such material. For this question can no more be answered by a reference to music's world-relation than a reference to the world-relation of verbal language can provide an answer to the question as to how literature can constitute a form of art.

3. Certain elements of such an answer are, however, contained in a third equally useful application of the lingual topos to music. In this case, not questions of semantic content or the world-relation of music are foremost, but rather of the "syntactical" and "grammatical"—and thus also, in a genuinely musical sense, already *context-forming*—aspects of music. The classic example is the idea of a "tonal" language of music. "Language" is spoken of here in *analogy* to verbal language, through a by no means arbitrary projection of syntactical, grammatical and rhetorical terms onto music. One need only think of such expressions as "sentence" (*Satz*), "antecedent and consequent" (*Vordersatz und Nachsatz*), "period", "cadence" (*Schluß*), (in the twofold meaning of *Schlußfolgerung* [conclusion/deduction] and *Schlußwendung* [final phrase]), (musical) "logic", "theme", "exposition", "development" (*Entwicklung/Durchführung*[10]) etc.[11] It is only here that the references to a *language* of music—as opposed to the world- and lingual/speech-*relation* of music—gain clearer definition. For one could understand the "language" of tonality, even though it underwent constant historical development to the edge of self-transgression, as a lingual background more or less common to the composers and listeners of the tonal era, which even individual harmonic and formal innovations nonetheless remained based on — much in the same way as literature also assumes a common lingual background which it can, at the same time, alter through its

---

10. Translator's note: Both of these terms correspond to the English *development*; the latter one is the standard musical term, e.g. as used in describing sonata form.
11. Translator's note: as a number of these terms only carry the verbally-related meaning referred to in the text in their German form, this has—in such cases—been included in brackets to avoid completely losing the original sense.

interventions. Beyond this, one could also say that the language of tonality, just like verbal language, has always incorporated additional semantic content alongside its syntactical aspects; what I have thematicised above as the expressive and semantic content of music corresponds to an expressive and semantic potential already contained, to an extent, in the language of tonality, even if this potential can surely only be fulfilled successively through each individual work and through the expansions of the tonal language effected by them. The analogy to language admittedly becomes more precarious when one tries to compare the context-forming potencies of the tonal language with those of verbal language, for these same context-forming potencies, which extend from the construction of "sentences" and "periods" to the construction of such large-scale forms as fugue, sonata and rondo, cannot simply be equated with those of verbal syntax, grammar and rhetoric, for the simple reason that these latter are not even *literary* forms, but simply textual conjunctions of any kind. The context-forming potencies of the tonal language, on the other hand, are substantially *form*ative potencies in a musical sense. One cannot understand these correctly, however, if one does not also take into account — as demanded by Schnebel — the formative potencies of a play of repetition and variation, identity and difference with a particular sonic material, and hence formative potencies of a kind not geared towards a *semantic* context. This becomes clear upon an examination of "classical" formal models such as the fugue, sonata and rondo forms: each of these formal types at the same time connotes a particular manifestation of the play of repetition and variation, similarity and contrast, of sequence and mirroring — in short, of identity and difference. This play of identity and difference, however, as one can see in ornamental figurations such as carpets, or indeed in the works of Morton Feldman which were inspired by these, sooner *subverts* meaning than *produces* it; in verbal language it would be rhymes, alliterations, word-games and other, more complex formal means of creating a literary context which correspond most closely to this play of identity and difference.

What is precarious about the metaphor of a tonal *language* of music is not so much the fact that the comparison between musical and verbal language — how could it be otherwise? — comes up against certain limitations; what is far more precarious is its suggestion that musical contextuality can adequately be understood in terms of such notions as "statement", "representation" or "communication". I will attempt to show later on why this is not possible. When one therefore uses the metaphor of a tonal "language", then it should only be in a quasi-Wittgensteinian consciousness of similarities *and* dissimilarities between musical and verbal language, so as not to fall foul of the assumption that music "says", in a different language, what cannot be said in verbal language — a suggestion already at the heart of the early Romantic idea that music, as the language of emotions, is a "richer" or "more profound" language than the verbal. What is misguided about this idea is not the suggestion that music "does" something which verbal language cannot, but rather the fact that in this concept the lingual topos — the analogy between musical and verbal language — is stretched beyond its capacity and the misleading assumption is made that musical contextuality is somehow analogous to the semantic contexts arising in — non-literary — verbal language; this idea was already rejected by Adorno, despite his theory of music's speech-likeness, and with good reason. At this point, I would like to cite a passage from an essay by Adorno on music and language in which it becomes quite clear that Schnebel's objections to the "lingualisation" of music are not, in fact, relevant to Adorno's position. He writes: "Music is speech-like. (...) But music is not language. Its speech-likeness shows us the way to its core, but also to vagueness. Whoever takes music literally as language will be misled by it. (...) Compared to the language of meaning, music is language only as one of an entirely different kind. (...) But it is not conclusively distinct from it as one realm is from another. We find a dialectic: it is certainly imbued with intentions, and definitely not only since the *stile rappresentativo*, which applied rationalisation to music in order to gain control of its linguality. Music devoid of all meaning, the mere phenomenal context of sounds, would be acoustically equivalent to a kaleidoscope. As absolute meaning, on the other hand, it would cease to be music, and falsely become language. Intentions are a part of its substance, but only intermittently. (...) Time and time again it shows that it means, and that it means definitely; the intention, however, is simultaneously always concealed. (...) In order to distinguish music from the mere succession of sensory stimuli, one has termed it a sensory or structural context, and in so far as nothing stands isolated within it, and everything becomes what it is in corporeal contact only with the nearest and in spiritual contact with the most distant, in recollection and anticipation, one can allow this statement to pass. But this context is not a semantic one in the sense instigated by the language of meaning. The whole is realised against all intentions — it integrates them through a negation of each singular, indeterminable one of them. Music as a whole rescues the intentions, not in diluting them to a higher, more abstract intention, but rather through invoking, in the moment of its consummation, the non-intentional. It is thus almost the opposite of a semantic context, even where it poses as such in relation to its sensory *thereness*."[12]

What is incorrect about the notion that musical contextuality is something analogous to semantic contexts in verbal language can also be clarified by reminding oneself how tenuous the language-analogy is to begin with: are we, in using it, comparing musical formations ("utterances") to those of everyday, communicationally-oriented verbal usage, or to those of literature? Any answer one could supply to this question must sooner or later lead us to the *crookedness* of the comparison: the comparison to our everyday, communicative verbal language is crooked because, in the case of music, there is no such thing as an everyday language beyond music as an art form (the only comparable thing would be bad music). The language of *literature* should therefore be the focus of the comparison; but here too the comparison becomes a crooked one, as the language of literature is no other than verbal language. In order to retrieve the comparison, we would have to return to the question of what, in music, is analogous to verbal language — and that means: we are starting to move in circles.

---

12. Adorno, *Musik, Sprache und ihr Verhältnis im gegenwärtigen Komponieren*, in: *Gesammelte Schriften* vol. 16, Frankfurt a. M. 1978, pp. 650–653.

(One could also describe the problem more simply as follows: literature also "does" something which communicative language in its ordinary usage cannot. But one would not say for this reason that the language of literature is a *different*—perhaps a "richer", or more "profound"—language to verbal language; for it does, after all, *consist* of words.)

It is nonetheless important to realise that the language-topos has sustained itself, in the syntactical-formative sense examined above, beyond the end of tonal music. This could be illustrated by some of the self-interpretations of the post-war serial avant-garde, in particular those of Boulez, where the overcoming of the tonal "language" is presented as the problem of constructing a new musical language—a new syntax, grammar and semantics of music. Mary Breatnach has formulated the role of the language-topos in Boulez' self-interpretation in the following terms: "Language and expression are inseparable in music. When the expressive possibilities of a language have been outlived, then the need for constructing a new language makes itself felt."[13] In this use of the language-topos, the early serial attempts—for example *Structures I* by Boulez—appear as attempts to construct a new musical *language* and not—as Adorno tended, at least at times, towards believing—as a threat to the speech-likeness of music. Admittedly, the hope of a new "language" of music analogous in its generally binding systematicity to the tonal language soon transpired as an illusion. Adorno was right in diagnosing the collapse of the tonal language common to all composers as a compulsion towards an increasing *individualisation* of "language" and formal construction in music. This insight, however, implies yet a further differentiation of the language-topos with regard to music. For it is now no longer a matter of something analogous to the commonality of verbal language—as was still the case in the topos of the "tonal language of music"—, but rather of the necessity forcing each composer to find a language of his *own*, as Boulez stated, on the other hand, in reference to Webern and his individual

---

13. Mary Breatnach, *Boulez and Mallarmé*, Aldershot 1996, p. 75.

interpretation of the twelve-note method: "'Finding a language', says Rimbaud... Without any doubt, Webern fulfilled this."[14] One could here speak of an "extension" of the language-topos in precisely the same sense in which Wittgenstein spoke of an extension of the terms "game" or "number": "We expand our notion of number just as we connect one fibre to the next when weaving a thread. And the strength of the thread does not depend on one fibre extending throughout the whole of its length, but rather on many of these fibres overlapping."[15] What this means is: Webern's idiosyncratic adaptation of the note-row principle constituted the invention of a formative musical syntax through which he — in a more consistent form than either Schönberg or Berg — fulfilled the possibilities of a post-tonal contextual formation in a manner that was at the same time highly individualised and also productive for the generations that followed. When Boulez speaks of Webern's *language*, this topos has now not only distanced itself from the analogy to verbal language, but also from an analogy to the tonal "language" — which had after all been intended as one *common* to all composers — to a considerable degree. All the same, we can — assuming we find the music of the late Webern at all "meaningful" in the first place — understand Boulez' "continuation" of the language-topos in relation to Webern's "language" without any difficulty, for the reason that figures of speech — such as when an artist or a philosopher is spoken of as having "found his own language" — from other contexts are entirely familiar to us. What is important is simply to remain aware that this is a "continuation" of the language-topos which would definitely be misunderstood by forgetting the intermediate steps that lead from the notion of verbal language to that of a "language" of Webern. The legitimacy of the language-topos with reference to individual composers — Webern, Messiaen, Nono, Kurtág or Lachenmann — ultimately always depends on whether the composers in question

---

14. Pierre Boulez, *Anton Webern*, in: Josef Häusler (ed.), *Pierre Boulez in Salzburg* (programme of the Salzburger Festspiele 1992), Zurich/Basle 1992, p. 77.
15. Ludwig Wittgenstein, *Philosophische Untersuchungen*. (*Schriften* vol. 1), Frankfurt a. M. 1960, p. 325.

have created something at once new and significant; and, if this is the case, then one can speak of the "language" of Webern in more or less the same sense as one also speaks of the respective languages of Shakespeare, Goethe or Beckett — except that this analogy can also never be more than partially correct, as the "language" of Webern, in contrast to those of Shakespeare, Goethe or Beckett, no longer assumes a *common* language (syntax, grammar and semantics). In the case of music, the "individualisation" of "language" in the 20th century is therefore once again *not* the same as the individualisation of language effected by such authors as Kafka, Joyce or Beckett. What is more important than the aforementioned boundaries of the analogy between musical and verbal language, however, is something else: what has meanwhile become clear is that the language-topos — music *as* language — can mislead us in a twofold sense: while, in the aspects named in points 1. and 2., we were faced with the problem that the language-topos cannot explain how a specifically *musical* context is possible, the problem with the third aspect of music's "speech-likeness" just discussed is that the constitutive *difference* between specifically musical context-formations and those of everyday (that is, non-literary) verbal language is lost from our view. This, on the other hand, shows that the reference to the speech-analogous characteristics of music is not sufficient if we are to understand the relationship between music and language. It becomes apparent here, I believe, that an image used by Ferneyhough of music as a "satellite" of language with an extremely eccentric orbit is ultimately more useful than all attempts to grasp music *as* (a particular) language. And what I meant by my reference to the latent intermediality of music (and all other artistic media), as well as to its latent *relation* to verbal language, was something similar to what Ferneyhough describes.

4. Before pursuing this idea any further, I would like to refer to an additional aspect of music (that is, European art music) which — albeit in a rather different fashion to the preceding discussion — would seem to support the application of the lingual topos; we are dealing here not with the notion of music as "speech in sound", but rather as notes on paper, that is the textual, the

"written" character of musical scores. After all, our concept of the musical work of art ("opus") grew under the influence of the notational system developed in Europe since the Middle Ages and — in close connection to this — the later development of tempered intonation. The European system of notation was not only an ingenious invention for the transcription of existing music; it took on a central role in the constitution of a specifically European musical tradition. This was not only because it rendered the composition of complex musical works — as we understand them today — possible in the first place, musical works which could exist as enduring objects in the form of scores, and be aesthetically constructed in the same manner as works of visual or literary art, regardless of the ephemerality of sonic events; it was above all because the textualisation of music simultaneously had a constitutive influence on the direction of musical development. For the textualisation of music effected a momentous change in its acoustic material which one could describe as a "trimming down" of this musical material to two notationally quantifiable parameters: pitch and duration. What was fundamental — as Jakob Ullmann puts it — was the "reduction of the musical text to a codification of its structure in pitches and durations."[16] The claim that this was not simply a means of selection with regard to those musical aspects — among the many dimensions of sonic events — which could in some sense be notationally fixed, but rather a change imposed on the musical material is supported by the problems which regularly impede any attempt to transcribe non-European music. For, in the case of such endeavours, one must always allow for the fact that a) the musical works being transcribed deal neither with precisely fixed pitches nor with intervals familiar to our ears, and b) that our notation is not at all suited to recording the characteristics which the identity of these works depends on. This is for the simple reason that the parameters which determine their identity are not the same ones as in European music — for example different sonic qualities, modes of

---

16. Jakob Ullmann, *"Ou Chronos"*, in: Heinz-Klaus Metzger & Rainer Riehn (ed.), *Musik-Konzepte* 100, April 1998, p. 116.

sound-production, the use of the voice etc. In other words: through the development of the European notational system, the emphasis in musical composition was instantly placed on those parameters which could be precisely controlled, as it were quantified through notation, namely pitch and duration, and also on the development of the tonal system implicit in this, with the corresponding focus on the harmonic and contrapuntal aspects of composition.

Jakob Ullmann has attempted to explain the stability of the European system of notation through a historical coincidence, and his attempt is at once witty and profound. The Byzantine emperor Constantinos Copronymos gave the Frankish king Pippin an organ as a gift, and this—according to Ullmann—bestowed upon keyboard instruments (later the piano, of course) the central importance which they took on in European musical practice, including composition. "The structure of these instruments", Ullmann writes, "proved extraordinarily well-suited to the structure of musical notation as it began to be established around the year 1000: this instrument permitted not only the production of exact pitches and exact durations, but the organ's design also made it seem natural to see in pitch and duration the deciding criteria for all that a musical text must necessarily codify. The organ thus not only became the yardstick for the codification of musical texts; its design and internal structure came to define the principal boundaries of what could be received as a musical text within the occidental tradition. In short, we can say: music is thus whatever has a pitch and a duration, and in such a form that it can be played on the organ."[17] (As mentioned earlier, the piano later superseded the organ.) In terming Ullmann's explanation both witty and profound above, I wished to point out that what is significant here is not so much the historical detail as the fact that the internal connection he points out between central aspects of the European notational system and the dominance of keyboard instruments in musical practice does indeed appear to exist, for example in the

---

17. ibid., p. 118 f.

sense that the compositional essence of musical works was for a long time defined as that which can be reproduced on a keyboard instrument.

Another integral factor in the process of coalescence between the notational system and keyboard instruments was of course the later development of the tempered system of intonation, that is the division of the octave into twelve equal semitone steps, which occasioned both a radical expansion of the tonal space controllable — in terms of cadential harmony — through modulation and also a consolidation of the dominant role of the piano, or keyboard instruments in general, as the only instruments within whose construction equal temperament could be "mechanically" implanted. For a notational practice centred around pitch and duration in the context of a tonal system of cadential harmony, such aspects as instrumentation, agogics, dynamics, playing techniques and the many modalities of sound-production were destined to be viewed from the perspective of music theory as a secondary, compositionally not "rationalisable" field of musical practice or sonic execution overlaying the "core" of the musical texture as defined by pitch and duration. This is also apparent in the practice of creating short scores as a preliminary stage in the composition of orchestral works and operas. In the short score, pitch sequences and durations are fixed; the full score is, as it were, the sonic and timbral "filling-in" of a "plan" or sketch which as such already contains all musical elements that are important in the structural sense — the orchestration of Act 3 of the opera *Lulu* carried out by Friedrich Cerha, for example, can therefore be viewed with a certain validity as the completion of a work by Alban Berg (as opposed to the "completion" of Mozart's Requiem by Franz Xaver Süßmayr).

Naturally, additional "parameters" alongside pitch and duration — timbre, dynamics, tone — have always played a deciding part in musical practice, and were accordingly — more or less explicitly — also notated: in the form of instrumentational or dynamic specifications, or with the aid of an increasingly rich vocabulary for the characterisation of movements and manner of rendition. And, since the 19th century — at the latest —, particularly in the cases of Berlioz and Wagner, one finds clear tendencies towards an incorporation of timbre into the core of the musical construction; it is revealing, however, that the music-theoretical world only became fully aware of the compositionally constructive significance which timbre had for such composers as Wagner during the 20th century. Even Adorno's *Versuch über Wagner* has been charged — and rightly so — with neglecting the constructive significance of the timbral parameter — i.e. the instrumentation — in Wagner's musical dramas, and criticising his musical constructions according to an ill-chosen model, namely that of the classical symphony and its formal principle of motivic-thematic development (a category clearly tailored to the two aforementioned parameters of pitch and duration).[18] It was only in the course of the 20th century — although not really yet in the Second Viennese School — that the dominant role of the parameters of pitch and duration was increasingly called into question; in the works of Debussy and Varèse, for example, as well as through the attempts in serial music to incorporate such parameters as dynamics, timbre, articulatory or instrumental techniques into musical composition in a constitutive, that is constructive sense — attempts which, to be sure, repeatedly encountered problems resulting from the mutual "incommensurability" of these parameters with regard to their "serialisation". It is thus hardly surprising that precisely the pitch-system of the tempered scale, which initially formed the point of departure for the many attempts at an egalitarian re-ordering of the various musical parameters (and which also constituted the last residue of tonal music), is now no longer viewed as sacrosanct in newer music. This is manifest in the practice of dividing intervals into quarter- or third-tones, in the attempts to overcome the octave as the foundation of all pitch-systems, or in all compositional approaches in which it is no longer the individual notes and their linear or vertical dispositions, but rather clusters and pitch-fields with their relationships or alterations that have become structurally formative, finally also in the constructive incorporation of

---

18. Cf. Richard Klein, *Solidarität mit Metaphysik? Ein Versuch über die musikphilosophische Problematik der Wagner-Kritik Theodor W. Adornos*, Würzburg 1991.

noise-phenomena into musical composition, sounds which were regarded during the tonal era as a-musical, or at best as inevitable by-products of sound-production.

In the various phases undergone by the dissolution of tonality, the traditional paradigm of musical composition—as determined by the connection between the European notational tradition and the role of keyboard instruments—has also been successively eroded. Not that it has vanished without trace; but one could certainly say that it was subsumed within a paradigm of musical composition where parameters and sound-phenomena not previously associated with tradition took on a central role, and where the once central parameters of pitch and duration were allocated a new one. The occasionally breathtaking developments in musical notational practice correspond to this; even though the classical notation of pitches and rhythms still plays an important part—after all, if one leaves aside electronic music or *musique concrète*, one still finds old instruments being used if not exclusively, then certainly *also* with their traditional playing techniques—, this function has been clearly relativised, and has as such become an object of explicit compositional reflection.

The internal connection between traditional notation and the role of keyboard instruments, it has to be said, permits a ideologico-positivist interpretation to the same degree as a "textualist"-realistic one. The positivist approach, which would presumably strike most people as absurd, has probably never been espoused by musicians, or advocated in its pure form by musical theorists (the philosopher Nelson Goodman provides an exception to this rule). I shall incorporate it here only as a form of contrast, in order to highlight the textual character of European music more clearly. The interpretation I would classify as positivist or ideological is one according to which, owing to the absolutely unambiguous relationship between notated pitches and piano keys, as well as the quantifiability of durations, a translation—controlled through calculation, as it were—of notation into sonic events is possible, and vice versa. Sonic realisations of a musical text with the aid of other instruments than the piano—an orchestra, for example—

could then, with a certain idealization, be understood in the sense of the aforementioned "standardisation" (through the relation to keyboard instruments). With this presupposition, one arrives without much effort at the distinction made by Goodman between the set of a given work's performances and that of its non-performances though the criterion of strict "compatibility" of the written music and its sonic realisation[19]; in this context it is irrelevant, as far as the notion of a clear "translatability" of the score into sonic events is concerned, whether one — as Goodman does, it should be noted[20] — views the instrumentational indications as an integral component of a musical score: the decisive point is that in every case the adequate sonic realisation of a musical text is taken as an objectively regulated and objectively controllable conversion of written symbols into sonic events. And this would mean that the precisely determinable "location" of any musical work of art is the score produced by the composer, and that the score's only musically essential aspect is the horizontal and vertical notation of pitches and durations, perhaps in conjunction with the corresponding instrumentational specifications. Even though such a work would require sonic realisation in order for it to be received as music, everything of significance for the "sound-object" would already have been objectively specified in the score. One need only utter this thought aloud for its absurdity to become apparent: it not only ignores the importance of that which is not notated, yet nonetheless defined by performance traditions in scores of historical works; it at the same time disregards, more importantly, the fundamental aspect of interpretation in the sonic realisation of written music. Yet perhaps this is an objectivist phantasm whose roots extend far back to fundamental aspects of European tradition, not only the musical. Naturally, other parameters than pitch and duration have always — and increasingly so since the start of the 19th century — been significant elements of composition, and indeed even these two were never thought of in an objectivist (that is, a precisely quantifiable) manner; as, however, the notational

---

19. Cf. Nelson Goodman, *Sprachen der Kunst*, Frankfurt a. M. 1973, p. 119 ff.
20. ibid., p. 187 f.

system applied to pitches and durations provided an ideal standard for a precise textual definition of sound-objects, it would have seemed natural for composers to attempt to achieve the greatest possible proximity to this ideal in the notation of the remaining musical parameters, and thus to find, with reference to these, a written delimitation of sound-objects for the purpose of protecting their works from the incalculable and wilful nature of interpretations. It is obvious that this is ultimately impossible; nonetheless, it is easy to see how the ideal of a fixed written score that needs to be protected from the whims of interpretation can lead quite smoothly to the notion that such a score is the most precise written documentation of the "intentions" or "sonic imagination" of a given composer possible, which must accordingly be taken as the norm for any interpretation in the sense of a sonic realisation. Implicit in this is the idea of fidelity to the work, which is based on the concept of an objectively correct sonic realisation of written music — with all the historicist consequences ensuing from this notion of work-fidelity.

By comparison, the textualist-realistic view of the internal connection between traditional notational practice and keyboard instruments would certainly recognise the "reductive" — and at the same time productive — aspect of the focus on pitches and durations characteristic of this notational practice, but also emphasise the textual character of European music established through this same practice, namely, the fundamental connection between the lasting nature of written scores and the necessity of their constantly being interpreted (in the sense of their sonic realisation) anew. It was only through its notational practice that European music was able to establish itself as a textual tradition comparable to that of other texts handed down in writing; and this in such a way that written works of music passed down through the ages needed to be re-interpreted from the perspective of each new historical situation, to be retrieved within the horizon of the given historical situation. From this viewpoint, the increasing efforts of many composers since the 19th century to heighten the precision of musical notation, even in those dimensions less open to notational control than pitch and duration, appear in a different light than in the positivist perspective I have just rejected, namely as an attempt to compensate individually for the loss of those principles of musical practice that could formerly be taken for granted, such as those still extant during the baroque era. During this period, composers could leave many aspects unspecified, as they could rely, as far as the sonic realisation of their scores was concerned, on the common conventions of the musical practice for which their works were produced. Since the revolutionary changes in European music since the First Viennese School, and with the increasing individualisation of the musical language in the 19th century, on the other hand, a more precise form of notation had to take the place of the collective standards of musical practice which had been lost, and this precision became all the more pronounced with the transition towards post-tonal music. It is surely of significance in this context that — as Lydia Goehr[21] in particular has pointed out — an emphatic notion of the musical work of art was only established from the start of the 19th century onwards, one which was associated with the demand for musical works to be received in concentrated contemplation as meaningful aesthetic objects in their own right; this constituted a historical change in the social status of music which accompanied the gradual development of concert life as we know it today. In contrast to Lydia Goehr, however, it is my belief that this historically-situated work-ideal cannot serve without further ado as the clue to a philosophical analysis of the work-concept as such; for, although music's demand to be viewed as autonomous art was articulated clearly for the first time through it, its traditional usage is at the same time burdened with various ideological connotations which I would prefer to avoid here from the outset. I shall return later to problems concerning the work-concept, attempting not a historical, but rather a systematic-aesthetic clarification of the work-concept as the conception of a musico-aesthetic "object". A work-concept of this kind would need to be equally applicable to pre-classical, post-tonal or aleatory music, as well as to music that breaks decidedly with the classical-Romantic work-ideal.

---

21. Lydia Goehr, *The Imaginary Museum of Musical Works: An Essay in the Philosophy of Music*, Oxford 1992.

My immediate intention in setting up an opposition between a textualist-realistic and a positivist-ideological understanding of traditional notational practice in music is a twofold one: firstly, the positivist model has never, of course, held any truth; musical texts have never determined their own sonic realisation, as it were, in European music; the necessity of an interpreting sonic realisation could, however, certainly remain halfway in the shadow of a musical pre-consciousness for as long as collective standards of musical practice could be taken for granted by composers. Secondly, the reduction of musical texture to the parameters of pitch and duration was never, even in European music, a reality in the practical sense; other parameters such as dynamics, methods of sound-production, or the introduction of the human voice, subtleties of rhythm, ornamentation and tempo, and finally timbre, have always played a more or less significant part — these parameters (with the trivial exception of instrumentational specifications) simply did not need to be fixed precisely in notation for a considerable time, as the musical practice in question, with its own inbuilt means for continuing tradition, took care of itself to a certain extent. This does not suggest, of course, that the primacy of the parameters of pitch and duration for large parts of the European musical tradition, especially European music theory, should be denied; nor does it suggest that we should doubt the extent to which musical structure was understood in terms of these two parameters in the European musical tradition. It simply points to the fact that the corresponding notational practice was also fundamental to developing a context of musical tradition which always encompassed those aspects of interpretational culture that could not be objectively measured. As soon as the musical text's dependence on an interpreting sonic realisation becomes clear to us, however, that is, as soon as it is considered according to the conditions of a hermeneutically-enlightened consciousness which has discarded the illusion of any text's "sense in itself", the question as to "what" or "where" the musical work of art actually is will pose itself in a new fashion.

This becomes all the clearer when one considers that, through the questioning of the traditional category of the "work" — as a musical context that is fixed in the written score, self-contained and dialectically-temporally organised—in some forms of newer music, the relationships between composers, performers and listeners had inevitably to change in a number of ways. Among possible paradigms for such changes would be the involvement of the performer in the compositional process in zones of compositional indeterminacy, the infiltration of musical realisation by improvisatory or gestural-theatrical elements, the development of open or "flexible" forms that delegate decisions as to the selection or temporal sequence of complex musical events to the performer, and finally also moments of a pure subsumption of the performer within pre-structured technical or mechanical processes. In all these cases, responsibilities are re-distributed between the composer and the performer; an element of musical *production* seeps into the sphere of musical *reproduction* to the same degree as an element of the performer's subsumption by pre-determined processes. On the one hand, therefore, the idea of a totality of musical meaning entirely determined in itself is called into question, yet on the other hand the "location" of musical meaning is redefined as an imaginary place in the point of intersection between composition, realisation and reception, that is as the site of a process that cannot be entirely controlled either by the composer or the performer.

Nonetheless, musical scores—like language-texts—always require interpretation; in the case of music, this means an "interpreting" sonic realisation of the written music. But, even if interpretation as the sonic realisation of a score is not the same as the interpretation of language-texts, there is good reason to refer to this sonic realisation as an "interpretation". For, like the meaning of texts written in a language, the content of all that is notated in a musical text does not have any "being in itself"; one can rather say for both of these that their process of being interpreted is fundamental to their being ("esse est interpretari"). We thus find an analogy between the musical text and *writing*; both attain being through a process of having to be constantly interpreted anew from within a particular historical horizon. At the same time, however, this means that the "being" of musical works is a substantially historical one; their being is, as Adorno observed, a *becoming*. It would be to misunderstand the application of the interpretational topos to music, however, if one sought to understand it *purely* in the sense of an analogy between the explication (as it articulates itself lingually) of language-texts and the interpreting sonic realisation of musical texts. For one would not even understand the analogy itself correctly if one were to neglect relating interpreting music-*making* back to a possibility and necessity of *lingual* articulation — namely, interpreting, analysing, describing and speaking critically *about* music — as an ever-present background, with regard both to the musical text and the "sonic text" resulting from its respective musical execution. This means that all interpreting music-making, which surely occurs often in a more or less wordless, mimetic fashion, and can be corrected through mere demonstration, is — in the same manner as musical listening — related much more significantly to a space of possible lingual articulation than the allergy among many musicians to speaking about music, for example, might lead us to expect. Only through this connection of both music-making and musical listening to a space of lingual articulation, interpretation and critique can music become an object of genuine *aesthetic* experience in the first place, and only thus can such normative concepts as aesthetic success or failure gain a hold in the context of communication, and of arguments over musical works and our experience of them. I had already spoken further above of a speech-*relation* of music; I had explained this musical speech-relation with reference to the speech-*background* of music (as well as the other arts). This speech-background of music, and thus also its speech-relation must now be illuminated anew by considering in what sense music's "being" and the musical experience are tied to possibilities of lingual articulation — to interpretation, analysis, description, commentary and critique —, in short: to possibilities of speaking *about* music. We are thus dealing here with a musical speech-relation in the wider sense of a connection between musical experience and possibilities, or indeed necessities of lingual articulation, of speaking about music. It is precisely the aforementioned interpretational topos that leads, in a certain sense, from the "speech-analogous" aspects of music discussed previously to its speech-*relation* in the wider sense, and thus to a new dimension, the fifth of those dimensions of the relationship between music and language mentioned at the outset. This could be viewed, to an extent, as the converse of the expressive, semantic and syntactical aspects of music discussed in points 1. to 3. I shall therefore have to return to precisely these aspects later from a new perspective. From all I have said thus far, it is fair to expect that only a more precise understanding of the speech-relation now to be discussed will also present the various applications of the lingual topos to music itself, as I have so far discussed them, in the correct light.

III.

The matter of the relationship between music and language shall now be addressed through the following question: why do we *speak* (or write) about music at all? There are, after all, entire libraries filled with writings on music produced by musicologists, philosophers, composers or performers, to say nothing of music magazines, newspaper features, programmes for concerts, etc. At the same time, however, there is a common aversion among practising musicians to speaking about music, aside from the practical necessity of communicating on the correct or sensitive way of playing a given piece, and in this latter context, experimentation and demonstration are often as important as words. But what does it mean to speak here of "correct" or "sensitive" performance? If all goes well, we might speak after a concert of a *grandiose* performance of Mahler's *Sixth Symphony*. Beyond this, it seems likely that every musician will admit that, in addition to rehearsing and experimenting, an examination of the score is important in order to grasp structural or motivic connections, the "sense" of the rhythmic, motivic, sonic or instrumentally-specific details correctly within the context of the whole. Naturally, language is required for this purpose: the language used by musicians, music theorists and composers to speak of musical contexts and details, of playing techniques and approaches. Many musicians' allergy to speaking about music relates not to this, but rather to a form of discourse that does not stem directly from an engagement with the work, with the music being performed—a mode of speaking that does not serve the purpose of "proper" music-making. But there are also the musical *listeners*—and every musician is at the same time also a listener. For listeners, the more they wish to engage seriously with music, the words written or spoken in programme-books, introductions or music-reviews can make an important contribution to their understanding of the music. And if they desire to gain a better understanding of what is being said or written, they will be forced to listen repeatedly—with the aid of CDs, for example—, perhaps ultimately even to study the scores before listening again, etc. An element of reflection thus forms an important part of music-making or listening, an attempt to grasp contexts and details *within* the context. And through this, language and concepts always come into play. Music, like all the arts, is directed at speaking, thinking animals, and the aspect of reflection and of grasping a formative whole that belongs to any genuine musical experience does not exhaust itself in the immediacy of playing or listening; it precedes the performance, and continues in the forms of interpretation, commentary and critique. As this applies not only to music, but indeed to all the arts, one could even say at this point that works of art are "shot through with conceptual elements" (Adorno)—a claim that seeks to oppose the notion that a work of art is something that exhausts itself in the immediacy of a tactile, acoustic or visual presence. This is not, of course, to deny the factor of immediacy, of involuntariness, of an "ec-static" experience of artistic presence; I simply wish to say that the ecstatic element of artistic experience—which is perhaps at its strongest in music, which touches us at depths, both of the unconscious and of our body in its affective and erotic entanglement in the world, which are normally concealed from us—is tied to an element of reflection, to the concentration of contextually-formative listening, if it is truly to be an experience that meets the work's own demands. Perhaps I can mention an experience which I often have while listening to the radio in the morning or the evening while awakening or falling asleep: I am suddenly electrified by music of which I have heard only a small segment, without even listening closely. It is almost as if I am simultaneously hearing a perfect whole in this short passage of music; and such moments of involuntariness, when sparks suddenly fly from the music, producing an involuntary experience of heightened presence, surely form a fundamental part of musical experience as such, in so far as one is dealing with an accomplished music; on their own, however, these moments do not provide a genuine musical experience, which is rather tied to the aspect of reflection and synthesis I have mentioned above.

Speaking about music has a different meaning if—as in philosophy—it is a matter of clarifying for oneself what it actually is that makes music meaningful to us, what position in life music (and indeed all art) occupies, what makes works of art succeed, and in this context also what and how works of art in fact "are"—neither functional objects nor statements, nor mere configurations of sensory material in time or space. I would think, however, that these questions are not interesting only to philosophers, but are rather inherent, in a peculiar fashion, in both the execution and the experience of art. This is particularly apparent in modern art, where the question as to what art is has itself flowed into artistic production: significant modern art, I would argue, has always also been a reflection carried out in the medium of art itself concerning the idea of art, and thus at the same time a critique of what has become—both institutionally and in society's consciousness—of art. I shall return to this later; all I wish to say at this juncture is that the question as to the idea of art is in fact, in a strange way, intrinsic to art itself. The philosophical questions I have just alluded to present themselves, to a certain extent, as much in the context of actual artistic production as in art criticism—and in the most pertinent way whenever the definition of art or of "art music" is at issue. This shows, however, that "art", "art music" or "work of art" are not descriptive or classificatory terms, but rather *normative*, and in this sense also notoriously controversial ones. One aspect of their deeper grammar is the fact that, strictly speaking, only successful works deserve to be termed *works of art*. I shall also return to this later on.

My initial intention was simply to show to what extent music is dependent on a field of (verbal-)lingual articulation, which means at the same time that a conceptual and reflexive dimension forms

a part of musical production and reception, in fact of music itself.
Further above I referred to the historicity of music in order to state
that musical works have a history of their own, within which they
can change, unfold, or even die out. I attempted to clarify this
with reference to the textual character of European art music:
musical texts — scores — must constantly be read, interpreted and
sonically realised anew from ever new historical perspectives, and
in the course of this process the texts themselves change. Jakob
Ullmann speaks of the "insertion of the text as a sonic realisation
into the respective present of each performance", and remarks:
"This process of inserting the text as a sonic realisation into the
respective present of each performance cannot fail to influence the
musical text. The experiences and patterns of explication which it
admittedly occasioned, yet which could simply not have been
revealed without the process of continuing interpretation, are
added to it."[22] The mode of being intrinsic to musical works — to
works of art in general — is therefore, as Adorno states, one of
becoming; and, in this process of the works' "becoming", language
takes on a central function in the forms of interpretation, commentary, analysis and critique. "But if the finished works only
become what they are," Adorno writes, "because their being is a
becoming, they are for their part referred to forms which embody
the crystallisation of this process: interpretation, commentary and
critique. These are not simply imposed on the works by those who
occupy themselves with them; they are rather the site of the works'
own historical movement, and therefore forms with a right of their
own."[23] I would now like to show somewhat more precisely what
this means, both in terms of the work-being of the works and the
aesthetic experience of the works *as* works of art.

I have so far referred to the necessity of lingual-interpretative
reflection in the context of music-making and musical listening
especially in relation to the structural context of musical works,
which entails a more "technical" — either theoretically or instru-

---

22. Jakob Ullmann, op.cit. (cf. 16), p. 117.
23. Adorno, *Ästhetische Theorie* (*Gesammelte Schriften* vol. 7), Frankfurt a. M. 1970, p. 289.

mentally-related, depending on the case—vocabulary. But the question is: does any such purely "technical" vocabulary, in which there is not already a sedimentation of extra-musical connotations, truly exist? As far as tonal music goes, I have my doubts: in the theoretical vocabulary relating to tonal music there is hardly any term which has not been "infected" with extra-musical implications. This begins with such words as "motive", "theme", "development"[24] and "exposition", in which the music is compared to the discourse of an orator, and continues in turns of phrase which refer to the formal, motoric or expressive character of musical works, complexes or phrases (from "andante", "waltz", "march", "rondo", "serenade", "Nachtmusik" to "morendo", "amoroso", "lebhaft", "stürmisch", "leidenschaftlich", "täppisch", etc.), finally culminating in references to ascending and descending lines, abrupt rhythmic or harmonic changes, "high" and "low" regions, "tension" and "resolution", to dense or calm textures, to "halting", "flowing", "whirling" or "clumsy" rhythms, etc. All these terms contain a metaphorical element which simultaneously relates the music to something extra-musical; in all of them one finds an echo, as it were, of music's world-relation. But not only that: with all changes in music, the appropriate analytical vocabulary also changes; terms like "motive", "theme", "motivic-thematic development", "developmental section", "melodic line", or the formal categories of tonal music, have little or no application in the context of most newer music. With the change in structural formations of context in music, the analytical vocabulary necessary for describing it must also change; this poses a challenge to musicians' and music theorists' capacity for the creative use of language and the formation of metaphors. I would like to argue, nonetheless, that this productive verbal capacity comes into play in completely different ways in the description, interpretation and analysis of music depending on whether it is applied primarily to the formal-structural, to the sonic or to the semantic aspects of music. I would like to provide an example: as far as Beethoven's piano sonatas —at least the earlier ones—are concerned, there is certainly a

---

24. Translator's note: cf. footnote 10; here, both German terms are employed in the original.

well-established vocabulary for its formal or structural analysis: sonata form, motivic-thematic development, exposition and developmental section, etc.; the point of a formal analysis, however, is naturally to unearth each of the individual concretizations, or indeed alterations, of these categories in Beethoven's musical constructions. The "formal" aspect of the analysis lies in its foregrounded treatment of such aspects as "motive" and "theme", "continuation",[25] "repetition" and "variation", "contrast", "augmentation", "diminution", "transformation", "recurrence", "harmonic disposition", "textural setting" and others, i.e. aspects which relate to the internal configuration of the musical material, not some form of extra-musical signification. I recall one episode from my days of piano lessons quite vividly—I was attempting to play the funeral march from the sonata in A flat major, op. 26, and my piano teacher, dissatisfied and impatient, suddenly exclaimed: "Now listen, this is the French Revolution!", and in so doing opened a field of associations which gave me access to the significance, character and world-relation of this music. It was an attempt to convey to me how the piece should be played, and at the same time to convey, beyond the structurally tangible organisation of musical material, what meaningfulness and affective content were contained in this music. One could call this a very elementary example of a *hermeneutical* interpretation focused on the content, sense or meaning of the music. Lachenmann speaks of the "aura" of meaningful music, and by this means—if I have understood his words correctly—precisely this meaningfulness through which music addresses us existentially and which, in my own terminology, also contains its world-relation. In this I concur with Adorno: "aura" was the term he sought to retrieve for contemporary art in the face of Walter Benjamin's affirmation of a "post-auratic" art. The "aura" and the "spirit" of works of art are ultimately one and the same thing to Adorno, and have the same meaning as their "content". The works' "spirit" is that which exceeds their material or sonic configuration, their object-quality.

---

25. Translator's note: in the original, the connection between the two terms *Setzung* and *Fortsetzung* is incorporated.

"The spirit is located within the configuration of what sensually comes to appearance. It moulds the appearance at the same time as being moulded by it; a source of light through which the phenomenon can shine."[26]

The question now is: what is the nature of the relationship between these two rather different ways of "understanding", "grasping" or "interpreting" works of art? I shall, if I may, present these in a simplified manner as the "structural" and the "hermeneutical" modes of understanding or interpreting. If my arguments thus far have been correct, then it cannot be entirely beyond the reach of lingual articulation to grasp the "aura", the "spirit" or the "world-relation" of works of art, even if the experience of meaningful music commonly renders us initially speech*less*; we *experience* its meaningfulness, but cannot say where it lies. The experience as such is a more or less speechless one, but it constitutes a challenge to our productive speech capacity, as none of the nebulously experienced meaningfulness of a given music can be brought into the light of consciousness without a productive lingualisation thereof. Roland Barthes expressed this in dramatic fashion: "As a body (as my body), the musical text is punctured by losses: I struggle to find a language, a name: *My kingdom for a word! Alas, if only I could write!* Music would be the force that struggles against writing" — this was written by Barthes in his attempt to interpret Schumann's *Kreisleriana*.[27] A further quotation will perhaps clarify how Barthes attempts to find quite general words for the significance and world-relation in Schumann's piano music: "Schumann's music contains something radical, which causes it to become more of an existential than a social or moral experience. Its Radicality is somehow connected to madness, even if Schumann's music is always 'well-behaved', in so far as it remains subservient to the code of tonality and the formal

---

26. Adorno, op. cit. (cf. 23), p. 135.
27. Roland Barthes, "Rasch", in: *Der entgegenkommende und der stumpfe Sinn*, Frankfurt a. M. 1982, p. 299 ff. See also Jacques Barzun, "Program Music and the Unicorn", in: *Berlioz and the Romantic Century*, vol. 1, Boston 1950, p. 194; also Barzun, "Music and Words", in: *Pleasures of Music*, London 1952.

regularity of melodic ornamentations. The madness grows very early on within the outlook and economy of the world to which Schumann entertains a relationship, one which gradually destroys him, while his music seeks to construct itself. [...] The world is not unreal for Schumann, its reality is not insignificant for him. Through its titles, sometimes through discreet suggestions of descriptivity, his music constantly refers to the most concrete of things: seasons, times of day, landscapes, celebrations, professions. Admittedly, this reality is under threat of dismemberment, of rupture, from movements that are not disjointed (nothing disharmonic), but short and, as it were, constantly 'mutating'. Nothing remains constant for long one movement interrupts another; this is the reign of the <u>intermezzo</u> — a dizzying notion, once it extends to affect the entire music, and the nature of formal constitution is experienced as an exhausting (though so graceful) sequence of spaces in between. Marcel Beaufils is quite right to place the literary motive of the carnival at the origin of Schumann's piano music..."[28] It is not the *aptness* of this description that is at issue here (though I naturally find it both fitting and illuminating), but rather the *type*, and its relevance: a description of this sort always pre-supposes the notion of formal relations or non-relations; but it discovers a significance *within* these relations and non-relations by which at the same time a world-relation is articulated in the music.

What I am proposing is the following: if one does not wish to confine aesthetic experience entirely to the moment of an artistic work's sensory presence, but also takes its continuation and elucidation in processes of interpretation and critique into account, as I have postulated above, then we must assume that the "meaningfulness" of works of art must also become an object of interpretation. The question then is: how can one grasp a thing, an object, that is at the same time "spirit", *both* as the one and the other, without entirely losing sight of the one *or* the other?

---

28. Barthes, "Schumann lieben", in: op. cit., p. 295.

IV.

At this point, I feel it is necessary to insert a digression on more general problems concerning the philosophy of art. During the course of this digression, I shall also attempt to approach gradually the specific themes and problems addressed by Helmut Lachenmann.

It was Valéry who characterised poetry as a sustained "hesitation on the threshold between sound and sense." I believe that this characterisation can be understood as a crude formula for that which lends all works of art their specificity, though admittedly the staging of this "hesitation" occurs from different points of departure in each of the forms of art: in poetry, for example, from the semantic material of language, in music from the materiality of sound and its structural organisation. In an altered form, Valéry's formula resurfaces in Heidegger's characterisation of the work of art as the initiation of a quarrel (*Streit*) between world and earth: "world" here represents those aspects of the work of art which provide an opening on the world and produce sense, while "earth" stands for the materiality which exhibits itself in that same work — sound, colour, stone, body etc.[29] Heidegger emphasises, however, that the materiality of the work of art is both the vehicle for its world-opening force and, at the same time, its opposite: the work of art "does not allow the raw material to disappear, but rather enables its existence in the first place"[30] — that is, in its asemantic materiality.

What both Valéry's and Heidegger's formulas lack is an aspect I have already mentioned, one which comes to the fore particularly in music: the aspect of structural organisation. Musical contextuality cannot be grasped without introducing such formal categories as repetition, variation, "statement" and "continuation", development, serialisation, contrast, augmentation, diminution,

---

29. Cf. Martin Heidegger, *Der Ursprung des Kunstwerkes*, in: *Holzwege*, Frankfurt a. M. 1950, p. 25 ff.
30. ibid., p. 31.

modulation, transformation, mirroring, etc., that is a play of identity and difference with reference to motivic units, rhythmic characters, sonic qualities, complexes and aspects, etc. Something analogous holds, however — I would like to claim —, in one or the other way for all the arts; one can thus understand Valéry's notion of "hesitation" and Heidegger's notion of "quarrel" as implying that each work of art, through its materiality and its formal organisation, both provides and subverts our access to meaning, that it suggests a semantic context to the same degree that it denies it. This is precisely what Adorno meant in referring to the "riddle nature" of works of art. "All works of art", Adorno wrote, "and art in general, are riddles; this has been a thorn in the side of the theory of art since time immemorial. The fact that works of art say something, while concealing it in the same breath, gives this riddle character a name in terms of language."[31]

Certainly, the formulas I have just referred to — of a "hesitation (of the work of art) on the threshold between sound and sense", or the initiation of a "quarrel between world and earth" through the work, or the formula that works of art "say something, yet conceal it in the same breath" — are grammatically opaque: how can a work, a product of artifice, a configuration of words, sounds, scenic events etc. be the location of a "hesitation" or a "quarrel", how can it at the same time say something and conceal it? The difficulty evidently stems from the fact that the idea of the work, its mode of being, is as yet entirely unclear. How and where "are" works of art? Are they in any way objectively "there", like things or events? In answer to this question, Adorno emphasised the "processual" character of works of art, by which he meant two things: on the one hand the process of their historical unfolding and alteration, as resulting from the historical changes undergone by their reception, but on the other hand also an internal processuality that contradicts their supposedly objective existence. He claimed this form of internal processuality not only for the temporal arts, as we term them, but for all works of art. How can one

---

31. Adorno, op. cit. (cf. 23), p. 182.

begin to understand this internal processuality intrinsic to works of art? It can, I would argue, only be understood with reference to the processuality of aesthetic experience: works of art are what they are, in the way that they are, only as objective correlates of an aesthetic experience. This aesthetic experience is a fundamental aspect of the works themselves, and this means that the question of their internal processuality must be referred back to the question of the processuality of aesthetic experience. But this does not simply redefine the works' being "ontologically", as it were; it in fact fixes it *normatively* at the same time. For, as aesthetic experience — as I will show in a moment — is an idea which can only be defined in a normative fashion, this normative aspect infiltrates the very idea of the work of art: only those works which succeed can, strictly speaking, be termed works of art. The idea of aesthetic accomplishment thus forms a part of our notion of art. It is the idea of art which is effective in every artistic production, perhaps never quite attainable, but effective nonetheless in the sense that the very idea, nay possibility of art could be at stake with every new act of artistic production. For the possibility of art is not something that can be taken for granted, not even as far as the socially-approved works are concerned: art cannot possibly be owned as property to be cared for and guarded; the fact that it is often misunderstood as such, and thus debased to a form of "cultural asset", is another matter.

I have just stated that aesthetic experience is an idea which can only be normatively defined. What I meant by this is that not every experience of art is an aesthetic experience, and not every effect which works of art have is relevant in aesthetic terms. An aesthetic experience of works of art is an experience in which there is an immanent aspect of judgement as to the accomplishment of the works in question. How can such an element of judgement be unified conceptually with the specific processuality of aesthetic experience? Kant was the first to find a suitable formula for this: the positive aesthetic judgement is the correlate of a free play of our cognitive faculties, that is of imagination (*Einbildungskraft*) and understanding (*Verstand*). Imagination and understanding are, for Kant, capacities for synthesis, for the creation of coherence

(*Zusammenhang*); the fact that they are in the state of a mutual free play means that their interplay as such — and not a definitive cognitive result thereof — is the ultimate telos of aesthetic experience. Certainly, Kant's formula remains opaque for as long as one neglects to remove it from the context of transcendental psychology within which Kant presents it. We find pointers towards this in Adorno's thought: art, according to Adorno, "is not, as general consensus would have it, synthesis; it rather dismembers these syntheses with the same force that brought them about."[32]

Adorno describes the processuality of art as that of creating and dismembering syntheses. After all that has been said, however, one must assume that the processuality of *works* of art can only be grasped in terms of the processuality of aesthetic *experience*. It is this processuality that — in relation to an aesthetic object — "brings about" and "dismembers" syntheses. What this actually means must admittedly also remain a mystery for as long as one understands aesthetic experience as something which exhausts itself in the immediacy — whether in listening, viewing or reading — of the confrontation with or performance of a work. What aesthetic experience is cannot, however, be adequately characterised if one does not see it in the context of its internal relationship to the various forms of explicit interpretation, analysis and critique in which it articulates itself, and in which — for the sake of illumination and correction — it prolongs itself. Interpretation and analysis are attempts to "synthesize", attempts to reconstruct that which provides the internal coherence, the significance, the specific unity of an aesthetic object. All that I have so far argued, however, points to the fact that any attempt at such an interpretative synthesis, whether it revolves around the works' meaning, their structural organisation, or indeed their "materiality", must come up against an internal boundary: a boundary where either the stubbornness of the work's material and structural aspects asserts itself over its semantic interpretation, or where the insis-

---

32. Adorno, op. cit., p. 209.

tence on and description of apparently objectively identifiable material qualities and formal relationships proves insufficient to account for the experienced significance of a work and, beyond that, proves implicitly dependent on "hermeneutic" anticipations of meaning. It then seems logical, however—in proposing this idea, I am following a suggestion made by Ruth Sonderegger[33]—to understand the particular form of aesthetic experience through which a work presents itself as "succeeding" (*gelungen*) as a play of interpretative syntheses which mutually support as well as destabilize each other; a form of play that does not aim for a particular result, but is rather self-sufficient in its orientation towards consummation and in its potential endlessness. This play of aesthetic experience is a source of pleasure in itself—this was already Kant's view; and we can now assume that the aforementioned "Dionysian" and semantic aspects and effects of art can only be ascribed to the works *as* works of art in so far as they can be understood as by-products of an aesthetic play of reflection.

There are thus no concrete norms or rules for aesthetic success; works of art are not produced or evaluated according to rules. In Lyotard's words: "Artists and writers work (...) without rules, they work in order to set up the rule of that which *shall have been made*." This cannot mean, however, that works of art are, to a degree, events in a space devoid of norms. Important works of art rather always have the effect, as Lyotard's words already imply, of *setting the norm*: they establish, as it were, a norm for aesthetic success which becomes effective for both artistic production and artistic reception. Artistic production does not occur in a normatively airtight space, but also always through engaging with the normative force of both existing and past works of art by changing, extending and breaking norms. (One need only recall what Beethoven did to the baroque form of the fugue and to the norms of fugal composition in "poeticising" the fugue and introducing it into the utterly foreign world of sonata form—and yet the norms of older fugal composition are still identifiable in Beethoven's

---

33. Ruth Sonderegger, *Für eine Ästhetik des Spiels*, Frankfurt a. M. 2000 (cf. in particular chap. III).

fugues; only by virtue of these can one speak of "fugues" in the first place. Nonetheless, the very *concept* of fugue changed with the "rupture" of these norms.) Every new work of art—if it truly is one—stands in a reflexive and critical relationship to a given world of aesthetic norms. It does not only have—and relate to—an extra-aesthetic context (as I have attempted to show), but simultaneously also the context of an existing art-world, which—in music through a relation to existing compositional problems, solutions and materials—it transgresses and thus changes. And a knowledge of such contexts can be important for an understanding of their constructive methods, just as a knowledge of their respective extra-aesthetic contexts can be important if their world-relation is to be grasped. Yet even if each work of art is substantially embedded in a historical and aesthetic context, it is, from the perspective of aesthetic accomplishment, at once context*less* and self-referential, a windowless monad, as its processuality is bound to one particular configuration of elements—sounds, colours, words etc. In transgressing, changing or criticising established aesthetic norms, it makes its own specific, normative demands bound to the aesthetic context, which it can only fulfil, however, as *this specific* aesthetic configuration of elements. In the case of accomplished works of art, this normative demand coincides with its own fulfilment, while in the case of some failed works, one could say that they do not meet the "norm" they have themselves set up, and thus their aesthetic claim and their achievement fall apart. In this sense, I believe it can be said that works of art must always also be judged in terms of their own self-imposed normative standard. This does not amount to a questioning of the general "norm" of aesthetic accomplishment which I formulated above; it is rather a first indication that this norm can only be brought into play correctly if the specific normative claim of works of art, which is conditioned by their relation to an aesthetic and historical context, is also grasped.

What I have described above as the potential endlessness of the aesthetic play of reflection could also be characterised, in relation to works of art, as their *internal negativity*—here the idea of negativity is intended to refer to the riddle character of art emphasised by Adorno, which demands a solution to the riddle with the aid of interpretations and readings to the same extent as through all of these interpretations and readings the riddle will always reappear. Pierre Boulez has formulated this point succinctly — from a slightly different perspective to that chosen by myself — at the end of his essay on Debussy's *Pelléas et Mélisande*. He initially remarks that a thorough analysis of a work, for example in preparation for a performance, can lead to the point where the piece "threatens to lose its magic." And he continues: "It then seems as if an excessive exertion of the intellect harms our spontaneity, and as if one would be forever prevented from still experiencing this work *naively*. However, with creations whose powerful radiance endures ("aura"!, A.W.), one could say on the contrary that the further one's insight develops the less one comes close to the origin of their secret." I have just attempted to read this relationship between "insight" and "secret" into the structure of aesthetic experience itself, an experience which cannot, as it were, ever reach the end of a definitive insight, a definitive form of understanding. And I have termed this the negativity of works of art — a negativity which is, of course, precisely the *positive* aspect of accomplished art and the sign of its independent logic and autonomy. I have so far characterised this internal negativity of art as the essence of its independent logic and autonomy in order to show that the "hidden totality" of accomplished works of art, namely that which enables them to be experienced as an aesthetically accomplished whole, cannot be concretely identified in any definitive sense, that it can therefore not be *summarised* through an interpretation centred around the work's materiality, its structure or its suggestions of meaning. Above all, no interpretation can do justice to this hidden totality by restricting the work of art as a meaningful whole to *one* meaning, one statement, one truth, by taking it as a symbolic whole which "shows" or "allows us to experience" something — in the same way that this hidden totality cannot be understood in terms of the intermittent moments of epiphany, of shock or intense experience. The hidden totality is the correlate of an aesthetic experience itself in the moment of its accomplishment, that is to say a play of contextual and morphological formations which reaches no definitive end.

V.

My digression concerning aesthetic experience was intended to clarify general aspects of the specific "logic" of artworks, the essence of their autonomy. Such generalities, which are characteristic of the majority of the philosophy of art, are surely in some sense unsatisfactory. Although I do believe that they are necessary for the purpose of outlining the framework for any reflections upon art, they certainly do not lead us into the specific artistic debates of our time, they do not explain what it is that makes the art of *our* time — and every art is first of all art of *its* time — significant to us. It is here that I wish to follow on from some of Helmut Lachenmann's thoughts.

Lachenmann has employed a different notion of negativity, or of aesthetic negation, to the one which I have just introduced, and it is this concept of aesthetic negation that I would like to take up in order to speak specifically of modern art, and at the same time also of the "temporal core" of art. Lachenmann refers to aesthetic negation in the sense of a negation of aesthetic preconceptions which have become sedimented in the musical material used by the composer. In doing so, he takes up *one* aspect of Adorno's notion of material: the idea that the material is "sedimented spirit", which amounts to "something pre-formed socially by passing through human consciousness,"[34] and this also means something loaded with significance, semantic contents and associations. Lachenmann demands of the composer that he break this pre-formation or "loadedness" of the material, for only thus can *new* musical structures be created, and our listening freed from automated habits. But whereas Adorno still spoke of the material's "laws of motion" — for which he has often been criticised —, Lachenmann only speaks, to a certain extent, of the material's "sluggishness" as the embodiment of the contextual formations, "meanings", associations, affective contents and listening habits always sedimented in any musical material, and which must constitute the composi-

---

34. Adorno, *Philosophie der Neuen Musik* (cf. 9), p. 39.

tion's *point of departure* which it must critically exceed, if it is not to be an eternal repetition of the same. As a composer, Lachenmann states, he is concerned with "undermining the old way of making music", and breaking the "collectively-radiant, false magic already bound up in the material."[35] The aim, however, is to explore new sounds and sound-relationships that have not yet become "loaded", to give new content to the débris of the old material, in short: to discover new musical continents, to liberate new expressive potentials in music, and to unburden musical listening from the obstacles created by habit and by the culture industry. "What interests me in composition is not simply the wreckage of destroyed sound-relationships, but rather the force-field of liberated and yet to be created sound-relationships."[36]

"Liberating musical listening", "breaking a collectively-radiant, false magic" — with these formulas, Lachenmann follows on from the great negational impulses issuing from the art of the 20th century, in particular taking up the impulses — albeit not the specific procedures or dogmatic ossifications — of serial music and its negation of tonal music's dispositions. What these negational impulses have in common is an aesthetic impulse which has, at the same time, a *social* dimension; it is a resistance against any inclinations towards a social — or, in today's terms, culture-industrial — appropriation, trivialisation, and levelling-out of art, that is to say a resistance against the tendency to use art as a lubricant for social reproduction.

Whenever Lachenmann speaks of aesthetic negation, he at once alludes to the great negational movement in the music of the 20th century, that is to the revolt against "tonality", and thus at the same time points clearly to the social dimension of aesthetic negation: negation of tonality means, first of all, a renunciation of the musico-linguistic, grammatical and formative resources of the world of cadential harmony, taken to its limits and — in a certain

---

35. Helmut Lachenmann, "Fragen — Antworten. Gespräch mit Heinz-Klaus Metzger", in: *Musik als existentielle Erfahrung*, Wiesbaden 1996, p. 197.
36. ibid., p. 193.

sense—also dogmatised in the serial music of the 1950s. But this negation also suggests a tendency towards a questioning of established forms of musical production and reception, and not least a questioning of all that has hitherto been associated in the social consciousness with music as an art form. The negation of tonality is not achieved with a single event (it has, after all, hardly even reached the music industry, the electronic mass media or established concert life yet), but rather an extraordinarily complex process, a slow transformation of the musical material, of modes of composition, reproduction and reception. In pointing out those forces which resist this transformational process, he simultaneously clarifies its social dimension: he names as the point of departure for his work on the material "the fixation of musical thought on the tonally-determined medium; the significance of this fixation as an aesthetic consequence of ideological dependence on norms, that have had their day, but still survive; the regression of the avant-garde scene under the influence of bourgeois musical attitudes; an avant-garde scene which, even in the provisional negation of tonality, still exploits those facets of tonality which promise easy communication; the questionable nature of political ambitions in music for as long as this music evades the problem of breaking through the aesthetic preconceptions of our society without affirming them again via the back door..."[37]

If I have spoken of a social dimension of what Lachenmann terms *aesthetic negation*, then the quotation shows clearly Lachenmann's —rightful, in my opinion—opposition to any rash equating of political and aesthetic negation: music can only be socially meaningful if it produces creations which are authentic in an aesthetic sense, that is to say by virtue of its aesthetic autonomy; any aspirations to effect social consequences must fall short or change into affirmation if musical compositions simply confirm the aesthetic preconceptions in which a social status quo expresses itself. What is hence socially significant, and "negative" also in a political sense, is in fact—paradoxically—precisely the retrieval of art as

---

37. Lachenmann, "Selbstportrait 1975", in: op.cit. (cf. 35), p. 153.

autonomous art. "Expectations that art should offer sermons, education or upbringing", Lachenmann states, "provoke allergic reactions from me. I hate the Messiah and love the Don Quixote ... and I believe in the little match-girl."[38]

Now Lachenmann has emphasised time and again that he is concerned with rendering the pure materiality of sound, its physicality audible once more with the aid of a new structural organisation of sounds, also ones previously excluded from music; at the same time, however, he speaks of a "reloading" of the material— conceivably behind the composer's back—with intentions and affective content, and like Adorno he emphasises that which "exceeds" the purely material sound-structure in meaningful music, which he—like Adorno—terms "aura" or "spirit". In Lachenmann's thinking, the polarities of "sound" and "sense", "earth" and "world", "materiality" and "meaningfulness" discussed earlier return in a different guise; this is why I think that my thoughts on the speech- and world-relation of music and the internal negativity of works of art have not become obsolete with the development of post-tonal music. In fact, one of Lachenmann's remarks in his *Offener Brief an Hans Werner Henze* points in the same direction. There he formulates the central question in his work: "How can one overcome a speechlessness which seems to have been hardened and complicated by the false loquacity of the aesthetic apparatus?"[39] Lachenmann's use of the speech topos in this passage is clearly related to what he describes — *and* calls for — as the "aura" or "spirit" of meaningful music; his polemic, however, is directed at the *false loquacity* of the aesthetic apparatus, and that is simply another term for what Lachenmann postulates as *aesthetic negation*.

Lachenmann's aforementioned question and the answers to it, which Lachenmann himself has offered in his writings and in his music, in fact have a precise correspondence to Adorno's reflections on New Music. For like Lachenmann, Adorno also understood—after a certain initial hesitation—the development of

---

38. Lachenmann, "Fragen—Antworten", in: op.cit., p. 201.
39. *Musik-Konzepte* 61/62, p. 18.

serial music and parametric thinking as a necessary step in moving beyond tonality. What Lachenmann describes as a "breaking" of a given musical material is referred to by Adorno as a "dequalification" and "delingualisation" of the same, meaning that through serial procedures the notes and their linear and harmonic relationships are removed from the semantic force-field of tonal harmony, and thus return to the status of mere natural acoustic material. Accordingly there were tendencies to incorporate spoken language itself into the compositional process as a semantically-neutralised sound-resource. Adorno certainly saw in dogmatic serialism—if it ever existed—the danger of a radical loss of music's speech-like character. At the same time, however, he recognised that serial procedures opened completely new possibilities for the formation of musical structures, possibilities which differed radically from those of tonal music, which had now been exhausted. For Adorno, this offered a chance to find new musico-linguistic possibilities, such as he subsequently attempted to circumscribe them—with explicit reference to existing compositions by Boulez and others—in his idea of a *musique informelle*. One could therefore say that the concept of aesthetic negation is also foreshadowed in Adorno's writings.

The question is now: how can the relationship between the internal negativity of works of art as expressing their independent internal logic on the one hand, and aesthetic negation in Lachenmann's sense on the other hand be defined more precisely? The internal negativity of art is another way of describing its autonomy called for also by Lachenmann as the correlate of "aesthetic negation" and in opposition to forms of political instrumentalisation of music. Nonetheless, the connection between these two forms of negativity has so far remained unclear. Why, one might ask, is the internal negativity of works of art tied to something like aesthetic negation, in Lachenmann's sense, as a precondition for their aesthetic success or authenticity? In Lachenmann's writings, one repeatedly encounters formulations which attempt to answer this question. They are characterised by an existential pathos, for example when Lachenmann demands of the composer an "existential claim of greatness, or should I say:

depth or spirit,"⁴⁰ which can only be attained if the music expels "the listener who confines himself to his idylls" from a "fixed space seemingly domesticated as art."⁴¹ Only thus can a confrontation with music become a new act of self-experience which breaks through social and aesthetic clichés. With this demand Lachenmann formulates an idea which has not yet found its place clearly in my "formal" characterisation of the *play* of art, namely that art can only be art by breaking out again and again from the shell of the art world which has degenerated into an "idyll", as it were questioning the established *notion* of art, the socially-established ways of *understanding* art, and the respective practices of artistic production and reception. Here too, Lachenmann stands in the tradition of the great avant-garde movements in the arts of the 20th century: these can, for the most part, be characterised by an impulse to question the traditional notion of art — an impulse, one should note, which is evident more or less latently already in the advanced art of the 19th century, in music already in Beethoven's late works. Since then, the notion and the possibility of art are at stake with each new act of artistic production. It is perhaps from this reflexive relationship of modern art to the concept of art and the conditions of its possibility, that the element which one might term the *specific* negativity of modern art stems. Aesthetic negation in Lachenmann's sense, which formed my point of departure, thus transpires as a specific expression of modern art's self-reflection upon the conditions of its possibility, that is upon the fact that each new act of artistic production must exceed and question an existing art world. In this sense, each successful work of art looks critically upon what has become of art, in particular upon the failed works of art; it is precisely through this critique that it also transforms past art, and in the best case even lends it a new relevance to the present. Asked what artists from the past had influenced his work, the painter Willem de Kooning replied that the past had not influenced him, but that he rather influenced the past through his work.

40. Lachenmann, "Musik als existentielle Erfahrung. Gespräch mit Ulrich Mosch", in: op. cit. (cf. 35), p. 219.
41. ibid., p. 225.

The postulate of the aesthetically new cannot, however, simply be equated with the requirement of artistic creativity, as obviously a necessity as this may be. It rather refers to something required *of* artistic creativity. A work can, according to Lachenmann, only be aesthetically new if it occasions a new self-perception and self-experience free of all clichés. This suggests, however, that in art, even in music, the matter of truth also comes obliquely into play. The concepts which Lachenmann sees opposing the authentically new are all concepts of falsity and inauthenticity: false loquacity, regression, the listener confining himself to his idylls, aesthetic predetermination as the precipitate of ideological dependence on outdated norms, etc. The postulate of the aesthetically new is therefore at once a postulate of authenticity; as the opposite of social falsity, however, authenticity has something to do with truth, not with any form of factual truth, but rather with truth in the sense of an authentic world- and self-relation, and also in the sense that truth is connected — not only in the operas of Mozart and Beethoven — to freedom. (I would like to recall in passing Schnebel's Cage-inspired attempts to develop new, anti-authoritarian forms of interaction between musicians/performers[42] and to thus open music at the same time to new forms of music theatre, to — as Foucault says — new "practices of freedom" *in* music: musical practice as a model of freedom.) But how can authentic art, how can music have anything to do with truth, if truth — as my earlier reflections suggested — cannot be the *what for* of art? Apparently only if art *comes into play* in a specific fashion in art; and this must be connected to what Adorno called the *temporal core* of art.

I said earlier that art always brings meanings into play through its "semantic" dimension. Admittedly, these are meanings which on the whole we initially lack the words to describe, and which therefore always also present a challenge for our productive speech capacity. Art can only be significant, however, to the extent that it does not simply introduce meanings, and with these also interpretations, but rather introduces them in such a manner that thereby

---

42. Translator's note: the latter term is meant in the sense of "performance art".

existentially significant contents—such as love, suffering, contingency, the fragility of the *condition humaine*, the natural, violence and death—are brought into play. In this respect, the world-relation of art is comparable to that of philosophy: in both there is a tendency towards addressing the *whole* of our life, towards addressing *our* world- and self-relation. And, if the specific negativity of modern art, that is to say its self-reflexivity, at the same time points to a perennial crisis in art, then we find a similar situation in philosophy after the end of metaphysics, after the death of God: both of these, philosophy and art—so it seems—can only survive together and perish together. To say, however, that, in the case of art, existential contents come into play in the mode of an aesthetic experience, means that their weight is experienced and suspended at one and the same time; on the one hand, the stakes are high, yet it is ultimately only a play; a play (that of aesthetic experience), however, which would hold no interest if it were not fuelled by the existentially significant contents it is playing with. In the context of aesthetic experience, we are placed within a reflexive relationship to the world and to ourselves, a relationship suspended in the balance, so to speak, between existential involvement and distance. And to say that, in art, *our* relationship to the world and to ourselves comes into play means that aesthetic experience, indeed art itself is nothing timeless, but rather something which can derive its own substance and significance only from the respective co-ordinates of a historical present. The aforementioned contents may be trans-historically significant in their generality; but their *specific* significance and the possibilities of their articulation change with the change of historical experiences and social constellations. Here, the aesthetic preconceptions which aesthetic negation sets itself the task of "breaking" are to be taken as blocking all that is aesthetically new, all that art requires for the sake of its *present relevance*. Ernst Bloch spoke in an appealing formulation of the "incognito of the now", which in music "in its unparalleled existential proximity (...) seeks (...) to achieve clarity."[43] The truth itself, which comes into play in art, has a

---

43. Ernst Bloch, *Das Prinzip Hoffnung*, Frankfurt a. M. 1959, p. 1278.

temporal core; it is the significance that materialises in the aesthetically new, the relevance of new experiential possibilities caught up in it. This also applies to the art of the past: *no* work of art can be present in an aesthetic sense without the ability to put down new roots in the hard soil of an immediate present. In this context, however, contemporary art takes on a decisive mediatory role: it sheds a new, a critical or a transforming light also on the works of the past; and it is the medium in which traditional works can renew themselves.

I have attempted to envisage a way of combining aesthetic negation — in Lachenmann's sense — with the internal negativity of works of art, their "worldliness" and their temporal core in such a way that two only seemingly contradictory requirements of art might become clear: on the one hand its independent logic and autonomy, on the other hand its being entangled in social processes in such a manner that works of art derive their existential content and their meaningfulness from the articulation of this entanglement, and from their reflection upon it. This "world-disclosing" aspect of art, however, is also connected to its *critical* potential. "There is nothing in art", Adorno said, "not even in its most sublimated forms, which does not stem from the world; but none of this is unchanged. All aesthetic categories are to be determined both in their relationship to the world and in their renunciation thereof."[44] In speaking of "renunciation", Adorno combines two dimensions of the negativity topos whose congruence had not yet transpired clearly until now, that is the internal negativity of works of art, i.e. their independent logic and autonomy, on the one hand, and their critical potential, the sting they direct *at* the "world", on the other. The latter one I have so far characterised mainly as a negativity related to an existing art-world: namely as an opposition — one particularly characteristic of modern art — to socially effective ideological conceptions of art, and also to the tendencies towards a neutralisation of art through the culture industry. To neutralise art means to deprive it of its sting,

---

44. Adorno, *Ästhetische Theorie* (cf. footnote 23) p. 209.

to change it into a cultural possession or a mere object of entertainment. Art's sting, however, lies in its breaking through clichés of perception and experience, or conspiring with them to question them playfully and change them, and in its opening of new perceptual and experiential possibilities. This relates first of all, of course, to *aesthetic* possibilities of perception and experience: art directs its sting at an existing *art* world. If this were all, however, it would lead merely to a fetishisation of whatever happens to be new. My reflections on the significance and the truth-relation of art should make it clear, however, that the critical potential of accomplished works of art with respect to a given art-world also implies a potential for *social* critique, as it is also suggested by my previous quotations from Lachenmann. Adorno's reflections on art always circled around this issue. At one point in the *Aesthetic Theory* he writes: "Whether art for its part becomes socially indifferent, an empty play and a mere decoration of the social machinery, depends on how far its constructions and assemblies are at the same time disassemblies, receiving and deconstructing those elements of reality which they join, out of freedom, to form something different."[45] For Adorno, the negativity of art lies at the same time in its articulation of the socially negative *as* something negative. Even if one removes this figure of thought from the quasi-utopian context of Adorno's aesthetics, it nonetheless remains as the realisation that art's world-relation at once holds a critical potential that affects frozen states of thinking, perceiving and experiencing with respect to both the self-relation of subjects and their social relations, and thus also — in theatre certainly more clearly than in instrumental music — a socio-critical potential, not least in dark times. As far as the necessary "sting" of art is concerned, the Austrian poet Ingeborg Bachmann once found a poignant formulation; it refers to poetry, but can be applied to music with little difficulty. In her *Frankfurter Vorlesungen*, Bachmann quotes a statement by Simone Weil: "The people need poetry as they need bread" — a "moving" statement, as Bachmann remarks. And she continues: "Poetry like bread? This bread would

---

45. op.cit., p. 379.

have to grate between our teeth, and awaken hunger rather than easing it. And this poetry will be sharp with insight and bitter from yearning before it is able to touch people in their sleep. For we sleep, we are sleepers, for fear of having to perceive ourselves and our world."[46]

The question is: how can art's world-relation and its critical potential be conceived of together with what I have described as the independent logic of art and the gratifying play of aesthetic experience? In considering this, one should first of all realise that the "negativity" of society claimed by Adorno cannot be taken as *the* (absolute) negativity of *the* society, whose articulation could perhaps be assigned to *the* arts. The world-relation of art and its critical content are rather — each as a concrete content — to be found in the separate works of art, accessible only to the touch of a penetrating interpretation and critique of individual works of art, as practised by Adorno, for example, in his interpretations of Beethoven, Schönberg or Mahler. At this point, therefore, philosophical reflection naturally forces a transition to a form of art *criticism*. Moreover, the weakness of any purely philosophical aesthetics becomes manifest — as, conversely, one weakness of art criticism lies in a tendency to detach itself entirely from philosophical reflection. At any rate: what can be said philosophically, that is in general terms, about art, is little enough, but this little is not superfluous because of it. I would like to illustrate this with reference to the notion of "world-disclosure". Art can be described as world-disclosing in so far as it opens new perceptual and experiential possibilities — not restricted to the realm of aesthetics —, allows in experiences of suffering, and anything excluded from established social discourses or not open to being thematised within it, lends a voice to those oppressed by society, in short: in so far as it articulates or thematises the socially negative, and thus at the same time articulates or evokes an impulse transcending this social negativity. This is not tantamount to broadcasting critical messages about an evil world, for a work of art is not a message.

---

46. Ingeborg Bachmann, "Aus den Frankfurter Vorlesungen", in: *Gedichte, Erzählungen, Hörspiel, Essays*, Munich 1964, p. 311.

Art does not practise critique by telling us how things really are, but rather by setting our thoughts in motion at the same time as opening our eyes and ears, and by occasionally heightening both reflection and complexity in allowing us to perceive and experience the ideological ossifications of the dominant discourses through its playful bewilderment of sense and the senses. Art's world-opening and critical potentials are one and the same. This sheds new light on the requirement of the *aesthetically new*, however, which is meant by the idea of aesthetic negation. For world-opening cannot be separated from linguistic, artistic, or practical innovation. Heidegger spoke of the "thrust" issuing from great works of art — a thrust which sets our perceptions, our concepts, and ultimately our relationship to the world and to ourselves in motion. In a similar sense, Ingeborg Bachmann says: "The transforming effect resulting from new works teaches us new perception, new emotion, new consciousness."[47] And with reference to music, Ernst Bloch speaks of "figures of transgressions in tonespheres;" we are dealing, according to Bloch, with "articulations of human existence in a developing language of intensity."[48] It is at this juncture that truth in art comes into play: it is not the *what for* of art; the manner in which — to use an apt formulation by Derrida — it is "inscribed" upon art, however, is the source of its potential for an *opening* of discourse and experience.

VI.

I characterised modern art above with reference to a *specific* negativity, namely its having become self-reflexive to a considerable degree as a result of its own increasing problems with the idea of art and the conditions of its possibility. The questioning of established notions of art tends, at the same time, towards a shifting of the boundaries defining what has thus far been considered art. In this context, one should also note the attempts at a negation of art *as* art — with the aim of "subsuming" it into life — of some avant-garde movements in the 20th century: even if these attempts were

---

47. ibid., p. 309.
48. Bloch, op. cit. (cf. 43), p. 1279 f.

damned to failure on account of their irreconcilability with the independent logics of art and politics, or art and ordinary life, they were certainly important as ventures against an institutional and commercial fencing-in and neutralisation of art, as gestures of transgressing an institutionally-entrenched practice and understanding of art. It should have become clear by now that the independent logic and autonomy of art I have defended here should not be confused with an inviolability of the norms and rules of play of whatever established art scene. A part of art's independent logic—paricularly in modernity—is rather still the constant transgression of such rules and norms, of the respective established understanding of art, of the practices of its production, transmission and reception. Such transgressions may often have a merely experimental character, they may not yet be art in the emphatic sense of the word, but aesthetically of interest as material explorations which promise aesthetically new possibilities. That which is experimental, unfinished, perhaps interesting, but as yet indeterminate in its aesthetic potential, the principle of trial and error —all this seems to belong to a greater extent to modern art than to that of the past; especially in music, for example in the various forms of electro-acoustic sound processing. To speak of contemporary art, therefore, also demands a recognition of the significance of its experimental environment, which is perhaps not producing "great" art as yet, but certainly testing new artistic possibilities and subjecting new materials to aesthetic investigation. I believe that the playful quality which belongs to this is a necessary condition of all artistic production. In this sense, I would also consider it necessary to comment upon Lachenmann's demand that composers should stick to an existential claim of "greatness", "depth" or "spirit". After all, such words as "greatness", "depth" or "spirit" are, as parts of our language-"material", highly loaded as codes of a bourgeois ideology of art which sought to place "great" European art music *de facto* within an enclave for the compensatory aesthetic-religious edification and self-affirmation of a bourgeois audience, an enclave for the good, the true and the beautiful protected from our evil, conflict-ridden and unpleasant social reality (which is, of course, precisely what Lachenmann does *not* want). This bourgeois ideology of art survives—in a depraved form, admittedly — also in the "serious music" branch of today's culture industry, not least in the festival system; any criticism of the culture industry issuing today from this breeding-ground of bourgeois art ideology is thus simply reactionary, that is to say *anti*-artistic. The mere concept of "serious music" already contains residues of this bourgeois ideology of art. "Serious music" today includes, especially in the radio and record industries, countless second- and third-rate compositions, as long as they can somehow be placed within the gravitational field of the "great masters"; its counter-concept has long since changed from that of *bad* music to that of the "lower" in music, that which does not *want* to belong within the reservation of "great", "deep" and "spiritual" music. On these terms, of course, one would already have to exclude many products of the New York School, as well as many works by Schnebel or Kagel, from the reservation of art music. In reality, I see their importance not least in the attempt to liberate music from the ideological ghetto of *false* greatness, depth and spirituality, which makes them prototypes for the many crossings and transgressions of boundaries in modern art. These crossings of boundaries have always existed, after all, with regard to the lower spheres of what one terms popular music, especially in the sense of an aesthetic transformation, redemption or a deconstructive play with its elements. This was not least one way in which social contents, conflicts and experiences were always able to find their way into composed music. I would argue that this is still the case, though possibly in a more aesthetically interesting sense than it previously was. Certainly the divide between advanced "serious" and "base" popular music has become progressively deeper in the 20th century, both institutionally and musically; it is easy to overlook, however, how independent some of the aesthetic developments taking place in jazz and pop music have been, and what musical potentials have transpired in the process. Certain aspects commonly associated with the stereotype of popular music have grown into an artistic sphere of their own kind, with clear artistic ambitions, and this sphere is threatened in its integrity by the music industry — which is at the same time its medium of existence, admittedly — to the same extent as all music today. What is conspicuous about the best examples of pop music is not only its innovative treatment of musical material, but also the fact that it is often saturated with reality, more deviant, more experimentally playful, and at the same time more "critical" than many second-rate specimens of "serious" music. This does not necessarily make them works of art; it does, however, explain why composers have begun to open themselves to the aesthetic potentials of pop music. A convincing example of this is, in my opinion, Bernhard Lang, whose background lies in the field of jazz and improvised music. In his piece *Differenz/Wiederholung 2*, based on texts by Deleuze, Burroughs and Christian Loidl, one encounters a music in which the immediacy of improvisation and the textualisation of music — which amounts, after all, to a thoroughgoing act of construction — stand in a new relationship to one another, and in which, at the same time, "serious" music opens itself to jazz and pop music: boundaries become fluid. In his music, Lang has integrated aesthetic potentials of pop music into a highly complex course of musical events; as a form of organized chaos — thus corresponding perfectly to Adorno's dictum that art should deal with introducing chaos into order — it manages to "speak" in a new way. "Greatness", "depth" and "spirit" seem somehow out of place if one considers the traditional connotations of these attributes — "obsessive ritualisation" and "relaxed, joyful wildness" would be more appropriate ones —, but I nonetheless consider this music authentic, also in the sense of the requirements postulated by Lachenmann. In short: I believe there are still other important and genuine ways to cross boundaries than those explicitly envisaged by Lachenmann and realised in his own music. The post-modernist slogan "anything goes" certainly is reactionary; what is in my opinion justified about post-modernism's insistence on the end of the great meta-narratives, however, is the fact that the state of the material has been pluralised, and that aesthetic transgressions in *many* directions have become possible and indeed necessary.[49] This applies to *all* the arts; it does, on the one hand, indi-

---

49. On the subject of "post-modernism" — or concerning the complexity of the "post-modern field" — cf. the title essay in: Albrecht Wellmer, *Zur Dialektik von Moderne und Postmoderne. Vernunftkritik nach Adorno*, Frankfurt a. M. 1985.

cate how difficult it is to continue producing art today, but on the other hand, I believe, it also points to artistic possibilities that are still far from being exhausted. To free these from being obstructed by aesthetic preconceptions is still, it seems to me, the desideratum which aesthetic and social interests converge upon today.

THESES ON THE RELATIONSHIP BETWEEN MUSIC AND TIME

Richard Klein

PREFATORY NOTE

The following essay sketches various theses concerning one particular philosophical and aesthetic problem complex: *music and time*. Its sections therefore occupy a common context, on the one hand, but are closed entities in themselves, and can accordingly be read independently of one another. I am aware of having left certain questions unanswered, certain conflicts and contradictions (especially between sections) unresolved, and also of formulating some ideas in a comparatively thetical or dogmatic fashion. In particular, the text does not achieve the goal it implicitly deems the central one in this issue: a mediation between philosophical thought and musical or musicological phenomenology. This leaves a significant gap, but also has — leaving aside the customary problem of insufficient space — an important factual explanation: I personally have not yet found any convincing way of integrating an analytical engagement with music into a discourse meeting customary philosophical demands without reducing certain works to mere illustrations of a philosophical idea, or conversely degrading philosophy to a speculative preamble to the "actual" musical matters. It is hardly the point, after all, that one can practise one discipline and a further in addition; it is rather a matter of clarifying how these two are, or could be, mutually related. From the philosopher's perspective, the difficulty lies not so much in recognising the fact that he cannot offer any terminological anticipation of musical analysis (this is common knowledge), but rather in being prepared, in the field of his own investigations, to accept instruction, even correction from the analytical side. The musicological "engrossment in details", on the other hand, must gain an insight whose justification it by definition rejects: the realisation that certain fundamental methods for understanding musical phenomena can be formulated — if at all — only in philosophicoaesthetic terms. Without doubt, the question of time is one of these; no amount of detailed musicological illustration can really do it justice.

This text therefore examines the problem from a purely philosophical perspective, while nonetheless asserting that its goal can only be achieved by devoting adequate attention to the other side, that of musical and compositional phenomenology. Without attending to individual works and specific structures, any discourse on tarrying, on freedom from time and the momentary quality of sounds remains confined to the consumer's viewpoint. Nonetheless, I wish to offer my thoughts for debate; even if philosophy cannot yet speak "properly" about music, it should have no qualms about being philosophy.

I.

> We write only at the frontmost edge of our knowledge, at the boundary which separates knowing from unknowing and *allows the one to change into the other.*   Gilles Deleuze[1]

In the context of *music and time*, one can fairly soon experience something interesting: upon revealing—the merest hint is sufficient—that one is examining this issue, and indeed why it should be this one in particular, the one being told—whether a layperson, a musician or a philosopher—usually shows a remarkable enthusiasm which can be interpreted either as a sign of great insight, or equally as a symptom of complete ignorance. There tends to be unanimous agreement that, in musical matters, to address the temporal category is to reach for truth itself; yet almost no one can say why this is so, or indeed in what sense it could be true.

What does this emphatic speechlessness express? What legitimate and/or illegitimate need does it reveal? It is my view that the issue as such arouses, or at least encourages, the desire for a liaison of extremes, for a liaison of sensory perception and "metaphysical" abstraction, of immediate experience and speculative thought, of

---

1. Original German quotation from: Gilles Deleuze, *Differenz und Wiederholung*, Munich 1997, p. 13 f.

the instantaneity of listening and the attempt to grasp at "last" or "forelast" questions. To postulate that the question of time is "the" one "it" all boils down to in music is presumably, for all the empty fury of such a claim, to secretly assert that life can be better understood by appreciating the implications of temporal representation in music. Those aspects that crumble apart into direct binary oppositions in conventional musical discourses (form and content, autonomy and worldliness) here combine to form an abrupt and harmonious synthesis, or rather symbiosis: in the name of musical time, it should be possible — in whatever fashion — to answer questions concerning a specific understanding of a composition's form to the same extent as ones pertaining to the experiential and semantic content transcending the mere sonic surface.

It would seem a natural objection, faced with so holistic an approach to the whole, that this argument is no more than the banal conclusion of a diffuse assumption. Instead of examining the temporal problem's various aspects in the concretion of their respective contexts, i.e. taking into account the specifically material and historical conditions affecting the structuring of musical time, one has here taken refuge in the mystificatory iconicity of *time itself*; this proves no more than the old wives' saying that a clear answer cannot follow an unclear question. It would demonstrate only a nonsensical urge to cultivate the danger of a decline into amateurism for the sake of mere affective stimulation; one should rather concentrate on confronting the plurality and diversity of temporal phenomena as rationally and analytically as possible.

This criticism, it must unquestionably be conceded, addresses a central issue. Time is a hydra, a many-headed monster. Any even vaguely serious attempt to make "music and time" the "object" of a theoretical and analytical examination leads automatically to a process of pluralisation and diversification comparable to the breaking of a dam. There is such a thing as the time of specific composers, of individual works, of typical forms, of fundamental material principles (functional harmony, metric rhythm, dodecaphony, serialism) or forms of medial representation (score, performance, compositional process). Alongside these aspects we find the historicity of musical comprehension, explication and interpretation. And, if one views the various manifestations of musical time as possible representations of human temporal experience and understanding, it is impossible to avoid being drawn into a further dynamic of polyvalency and having thus to distinguish between lived and experienced time, between individual temporal experience and the social constitution of time, and between the time-span of the mortal subject and the terrestrial/cosmic temporal horizon in which the former category is, so to speak, embedded. The question is: how can such an excess of multiplicity and diversity possibly be understood — in a manner that is productive, i.e. removed from any naive, unbroken totalisation — as a unity, or at least with regard to a possible unity?

The opposite stance to such a totalisation — let us term it, for the sake of simplicity, the "post-metaphysical" one — is therefore profoundly justified. It avoids seeking totality or unity (of time), as it considers these questions either undecided or as lacking sufficient musical pertinence — or perhaps because it simply does not feel responsible, or at least prepared, for the satisfaction of holistic or religious needs. It also reminds the more speculative philosophy that this latter domain exists within a world shaped *a priori* by science, and must accordingly confront the issue of scientific research if it is to continue being philosophy. It thus additionally forces its opponents to meet a standard of argumentation which can only be dispensed with at the cost of descending to the "a-method of intuition and enthusiasm" (Hegel).

There are, however, two opposed philosophical virtues: alongside that of precise research into empirical or linguistic facts, the virtue of stretching the limits of that which is conceivable and verifiable while at the same time maintaining the connection to them *without*— as with popular holistic approaches — merely separating the resulting problems from any contexts of rational justification or phenomenological analysis. What this means is that everything depends on *how* one deals with "metaphysical" ideas, motives and demands, not on *whether* one does this or not.

In the light of what has been said so far, a certain restraint in dealing with the *singulare tantum* of *time itself* seems as obvious and proper as clinging to criteria or dictates opposing the dispassionate ignorance — which denies the existence of any conflict — towards unity and integration that characterises a significant part of our scattered "postmodern" culture. Though we, as speaking animals, are denied the ability to establish a harmony between temporal unity and the multiplicity of temporal forms in a closed, "tonal" systematic order, this is no adequate reason to entirely relinquish one's demand for a mediation between divergent elements in a fit of ill-conceived self-denial. When dealing with questions such as those examined here, it is vital to prevent not only a diffusion of problems in the name of a colourful plurality and particularity, but equally what Benjamin referred to as the "greedy urge for the great whole", a phrase he applied to any manifestation of single-minded, straightforward fundamentalist philosophy.

When, for example, Georg Picht states that music is a representation *of* time, i.e. a "transcendental phenomenon" embodying the *phenomenality* of time as such,[2] then such a claim already poses problems simply because the identity-system found in Schelling's early work, which forms a part of its notional background (art as the "*organon* of philosophy"), can, in the conceptual horizon of the present, no longer be accepted without reservations. What Picht means is firstly this: time is the pre-requisite for the possibility of representation as such, and consequently also for representation in philosophical terms. And secondly: music presents time in particular as the univeral *a priori* from which and through which representation and philosophy can be attained in the first place. It enables us to experience *purely* that which conditions all experience, it speaks truthfully of time for all the perspectival and interpretative fractures it is faced with. This smacks of emphatic artistic idealism that not only places itself *a priori* above all scientific research, but also opposes every hermeneutical variety of verification or falsification. How can one, in the light of all this, speak of individual phenomena without relying, generally speaking, on a foregone conclusion? Philosophical speculation seems to remind us here of a hedgehog which the musical work in the form of a

---

2. Cf. Georg Picht, "Grundlinien einer Philosophie der Musik", in: *Wahrheit— Vernunft— Verantwortung. Philosophische Studien*, Stuttgart 1969, pp. 408–426. On the concept of art as a "transcendental phenomenon" cf. Picht, *Kunst und Mythos*, Stuttgart[4] 1993, especially p. 210 ff., also the text by Albrecht Wellmer in this volume.

hare cannot defeat, as it occupies both the entrance and the exit of the entire thought-process.

All the same, a verdict would be both unjust and counter-productive; for it is unnecessary to question the validity of a "transcendental philosophy of the senses" per se, simply because the effusive form imposed on it by Romantic idealism, which Picht and, in different ways, Adorno and Heidegger sought to expand upon, failed. Certainly, the impermissibility of any attempt to rehabilitate or re-animate this romanticism, with all its fantasies of salvation and deliverance, is obvious. But why should this apply equally to both the "weak" and the "critically considered" versions of this "transcendental philosophy?" Would not whatever remained automatically amount to a mere descriptivism of countless temporal forms which no one can seriously desire? In my opinion, it is precisely the point to present and analyse musical works as media which do not simply show or express this or that temporal form or historical character, but rather offer insights into the conditions under which such forms and characters can ensue. But: such "ensuing conditions" *do not imply any foundation in a truth of emphatic timelessness or meta-temporality, but rather a basis comprising the historical comprehension, conception, experience and construction of time.* It would be quite true to claim that music deals in essence with the production of temporal figures and figurations from acoustic materials, that it expresses different courses of movement and points of repose in all their diversity, that it articulates the passage of time in the most complex fashion through tempo and rhythm, acceleration and deceleration, stasis and abruptness. I would add: all this is true, but... it is not enough. *All temporal articulation in music revolves also around integrating that which is articulated, and understanding this integration. Every musical work of art can be seen as a reflexive representation — i.e. one that creates both distance and leeway — of what it means to be within time, to constantly shatter into the disparity of its dimensions and, at the same time, be constrained again and again to reassemble these shards as a unity.* This by no means suggests that the limited span of human life is music's ultimate standard, only that music presents time as a medium in which the inner historicity of subjective existence and the natural historical space of the world are both *situated. And: it is a vehicle for both carrying out and expressing the conflicts between the two aspects.*[3]

The question is, of course: does this hypothesis not for its part take on the hedgehog's role, which had only just been discarded, and once again classify the genuine structural problems of music, both of composing and of listening, in the name of an *a priori* philosophical construction? I would argue that it does not, provided one a) gives its sense a direction decidedly critical of idealism, and b) binds its theoretical status to an increased plausibility through phenomenological analysis. To what degree the theory of temporal understanding in/of music I have outlined is productive is something which cannot be established in a philosophically-immanent manner.

This is addressed to metaphysical and post-metaphysical schools of thought alike. It is currently considered "obsolete" to attempt breathing down the non-identical neck of artistic phenomena with generalised philosophical terms. This sometimes allows one to forget that precisely such separatist reactions against the "great philosophical tradition" can remain fixated upon that which they take such pains to avoid. At least, I can find no other explanation for the current abundance of those who preach a radical autonomy of all things aesthetic, and see literally any more speculative way of examining works of art as an imposition, an appropriation for other purposes. Is this not a poor form of abstraction? Can one reasonably present the defence of art's particularity against the generality of philosophy as a general philosophical argument without the interpretation of concrete phenomena to support it? I would argue that one cannot. One should rather be able to show precisely where, why and with what degree of systematic consistency (or indeed randomness) philosophy fails to do art justice,[4]

---

3. I have made a first attempt to verify this speculative notion in the context of a precise phenomenon in: "Gebrochene Temporalität: Die Revolution der musikalischen Zeit in Wagners "Ring" — speziellem Ohr für die "Götterdämmerung", in: Richard Klein / Staatsoper Stuttgart (ed.), *Narben des Gesamtkunstwerks: Wagners "Ring des Nibelungen"*, München 2001.
4. Cf. the examinations of Adorno's work on musical material in: Richard Klein & Claus-Steffen Mahnkopf (ed.), *Mit den Ohren denken. Adornos Philosophie der Musik*, Frankfurt a. M. 1998.

rather than dogmatically insisting that art and philosophy are two entirely different things.

Naturally, the history of philosophical aesthetics can — and with good reason — be told as the history of its object's terminological dominance; this is a valid claim. But it need result neither in the strict separation of speculation and phenomenology nor in the retreat to a status of autonomy which sees in any "terminological working-out" simply a means of ignoring the wealth and value of all that self-contained aesthetic radiance has to offer. If the passion among philosophers for aesthetic autonomy assumes such an ossified and defensive stance, it sooner demonstrates their own ideological confinement than the particularity they wish to propagate. In this sense, the amateur's universalist enthusiasm has its value, sensing as it does something which, often enough, professional theorists wrongfully consider beneath them.

II.

We should distinguish between coping with and representing time. *Coping with time* here connotes what Theunissen refers to in saying: "What definitely comes first is time, and then whatever we make of it."[5] Coping with time relates to a fundamental *a priori* state of *being in the world* which we are exposed to, regardless of our personal will. In this sense one is forced to "cope" with something which in technical, methodical or instrumental terms can precisely not be coped with. The central issue is that time always "is", that it constantly follows those who attempt to grasp it practically, reflexively or musically; we are faced with its ontological priority over subjective intentions, plans and projects, with the embedding of our finite life-span in infinite cosmic time and our inability either to elude or grasp this contingency. We must define our position in relation to this, we must react to and deal with it; even if we desired to do otherwise, we could not, and it is precisely to this practical compulsion that our notion of coping with time alludes. It emphasises the mutual entanglement of aesthetic and

---

5. Cf. Michael Theunissen, *Negative Theologie der Zeit*, Frankfurt a. M. 1991 (sleeve note).

existential, of musical and social perspectives, it seems to serve as a reminder that the internal autonomy of musical works feeds on practical connections to the world, that without these it would be damned to remain an an autonomist kaleidoscope, a non-committal play of technical prowess. There is an unstable, asymmetrical and insolubly conflict-ridden interplay of art and life, in Nietzsche's sense, affecting all this; the term continues to apply to something incompatible with classicist notions of harmony, substance or work-identity.

Temporal representation, on the other hand, implies that whatever is of utmost ontological priority can only indirectly and impurely be accessed and understood. "For us" there is no such thing as time "as such", only outlines or transcriptions of a nonexistent original that overlap and penetrate, in part even obstruct each other. The necessity of representation, and thus also of interpretation, is the detour characteristically taken by a temporal ontology that remains entangled in the task of interpretation. Yet binding this temporal understanding to an interpretative ontology does not seek to imply a human preoccupation with symbolic forms and systems, but rather respects the irreducible priority of time "as such", which does not and cannot exhaust itself in the forms of sense we have interpreted. If it is time that comes first, and what we make of it only after that, then whatever we make of it is not only externally shaped by "time itself", it indeed only comes into being in its light — as an ensemble of forms serving the purpose, in whatever way, of *making* "it" *apparent*. Time is no object that exists, but rather an area that is only experienced in the process of interpretation. At the same time, however, this experience cannot be reduced to "ontical" explicatory attempts; it rather retains its connection to an "ontological" purpose that precedes it. Any critical hermeneutics must be capable of combining ontological *and* constructivist thought; it must no more confine time to a subjective schematic order than it should cultivate the illusion of an "unadulterated phenomenality" of that which it views as the "true" nature of time.

I would argue that music — or, to be precise, occidental music — could be said to enjoy/have enjoyed a certain privilege, namely that of depicting the interweaving of ontological priority and hermeneutical detours, the negotiation between an unattainable *a priori* and a constructive temporal integration, and of furthering — in whatever manner — our awareness of this.

To be privileged is not to be exclusive; it can be shown that temporal structures verifiably present in musical works or forms are also significant in other arts. It would be premature, however, to conclude from this that such structures are only of subordinate relevance, that they do not access the innermost core of music's instinct need for autonomous validity. Unquestionably, there are certain analogies, for example, between sonata form and the *Bildungsroman:* both revolve around the communication of time and identity, both deal with the process of self-becoming or self-realisation of a subject, with his distraction through conflicts and collisions on the one hand, and on the other hand the return to his own self from this state of estrangement. One can show how this model historically reflects the emergence of "bourgeois emancipation" in the 18th century — and equally its problematisation and self-retraction in the 19th. Yet as deeply as one might engross oneself in such analogies, there remains the fundamental difference between a temporality at least substantially co-thematicised by the symbolic order of language and one that constitutes itself in the medium of sound itself — and which must indeed do so, for want of a discursive frame of reference of its own. It is no coincidence that philosophers from Augustine to Bergson and Husserl have tried time and again to grasp the problem of time's "abstraction"[6] through the example of a melody's transience. Music seems capable, *due to* — not in spite of — its "a-terminological" nature, of enabling us to experience time's horizon, its sensual *a priori* status in relation to all events taking place "within" it, and thus of attaining a representation of historical forms of human understanding — both of the self and the world — which might otherwise, without music, remain entirely inaccessible to both knowl-

---

6. Translator's note: it should be borne in mind that the original term *Ungegenständlichkeit* constitutes a negation of the *Gegenstand*, the object; in order to avoid confusion, however, the more misleading literal translation *non-objectivity* has been avoided.

edge and explication. To free "transcendental philosophy of the senses" from the forms of Romantic hyperbole applied to it should, therefore, not mean to entirely ignore music's proximity to speculative abstraction.[7] Such abstract questions as those concerning the relationship between presence and progression, memory and space, intensive and extensive time, or how the "subject" deals with loss, finitude, boundary and utopia etc., can ostensibly be articulated in a comparitively definite and structurally-related fashion precisely in music, as they cannot even be tempted to hide behind objective, empirical or discursive substance.

For one thing, music's relation to the world can only reveal itself in and through its specific forms and modes of temporal integration; in contrast to literary or poetic material, that of music is not *eo ipso* moulded by its connection to linguistic meaning, and in this sense it is, in its pure acoustic materiality, a-linguistic and therefore a-semantic. Furthermore, this relation to the world is more than a mere result of articulation and integration; for the medium through which our experience can gain access to it in the first place is, at the same time, anticipated by it. The material's a-semanticity by no means vanishes in the wake of the integration of temporal relations; it indeed continues to be present, even in these relations' most highly-reflected forms. Temporal representation in music is not simply the articulation and integration of time, but always additionally a discovery of the grounds for their

---

7. Hegel, who — contrary to popular opinion — did not naturally discriminate against "absolute music", was understandably disturbed by this. He begins by demonstrating that music can only bring the structure of subjectivity itself, of the "*Geist*", to the surface by means of its sonic mediality. Strictly speaking, he should consequently have applied to it the predicate of the "highest" form of art. An understanding of speculation, however, does not permit this. His interpretation of poetry in the third part of the *Vorlesungen zur Ästhetik* is, in its outrageous obliviousness to sound, no mere peripheral accident, but rather an expression of the compulsion to prevent a metaphysical elevation of music akin to those practised by Schopenhauer and the Romantics. Certainly, this has its justification; the Romantic construction of music as a "countersphere" to "rationale" is no less blind and contrived than a reduction of the sonic medium to a mere preliminary to speculative spiritual transcendence. One should insist, in opposition to Hegel, that occidental musical forms contain, in terms of temporal understanding, a "transcendental" force of penetration and representation which cannot be overtaken by any kind of philosophical terminology.

existence. To speak here of grounds or purpose is not to imply any "metaphysically" self-contained foundation, any presence of truth itself, any chronic manifestation of sense, but rather something like the following: a core that closes itself up, a foundation which, precisely under the strain of rational shaping, approaches obfuscation or indeed desolation, the meaningless converse of all meaningfully crafted time — and at the same time a non-entity that allows the apparation to stand out, and thus to appear.

It is not least a matter of preserving time from a "Platonist" reduction to pure negativity, or at least recognising within it *also* the leeway which enables us to penetrate and craft it, to a certain extent even to transcend it, and thus to deal with its irreconcilable otherness in forms and methods of infinite freedom. To this degree, Heidegger's "universalisation and affirmation" (Theunissen) has the last word. Time should not, of course, be suppressed or trivialised as the source of suffering; but no more can it be reduced to a transience in the sense of the inexorable flow of time as such. This insight takes on a complementary relation to the knowledge of its own negative might.

Time can only pass in relation to a present that endures, that remains. It is an oversight to constantly perceive only the elusiveness of that which has just appeared: one must at the same time recognise the permanence of the medium in which this emergence and withdrawal occur. This constancy does not transform a negative into a positive, it is not "affirmative", it neither consoles us in the loss occasioned by this disappearance nor offers us refuge from the abysmal future; it simply *exists*. Even there, however, it exists not as the stable continuity of a spirit or of "consciousness itself", but rather as the space which enables transience, irreversibility, temporal flow etc. to be experienced and understood as these in the first place — even if, for its part, it is dominated by absence and deprivation. The unstable present is not simply a mode of time, but rather the very basis, i.e. the nullified basis, for any temporal experience at all.

The problem in question becomes clearer if one reflects upon the context encompassing music and sound, or music and listening. It is not without reason that Georg Picht, alluding to Nietzsche, attempts to localise — above all in the sounds themselves — the "mythical" dimension of musical experience.[8] Sounds, he argues, are not things and objects, but rather forces and energies. As listeners, we feel ourselves placed within a medium whose suspended, oscillating phenomenality surrounds us as a distant atmospheric shell to the same extent that it confronts us suddenly and uncontrollably, without any of this distance. What is visible is present in every contoured shape, it has its place — visible and foreseeable from a distance — within space, i.e. the *visual space*. In relation to this, the forces and energies of the *sound*-space are lacking in contours, as they are invisible; they elude all the dictates of examination, presence and form, they occupy no position that could be precisely located as such, their event-structure is radically discontinuous, yet at the same time moulded into the distance, at least without a homogeneous or unifying existential foundation. The eye perceives "world" at every moment from a particular direction, it must carry out successive movements in order to view complex visual spaces; corresponding to its "spiritual nature" we therefore find not least sequences of cause and effect. What we hear, on the other hand, comes over or at us from all directions. In any case, the eye, even at its contemplative remove from the object-world, is characterised by an active approach to it: one has to open it, one must lift the concealing eyelid and turn one's attention to the impressions gained through it. By comparison, the ear is defined by an irreversibly profound passivity or mediality that exposes it — more or less unprotected — to the sonic impressions, effects and stimuli that assault it from all sides.

This phenomenal force of the acoustic realm, however, is not equivalent to a musical structure. But all musical structure issues from the fluid of this force and remains bound up in it: even the most concentrated of symphonic developmental forms arises from the tumult of chaotic sound-events, and the whole processual or "teleological" point of its internal organisation would be nothing without this confusion among the elemental discontinuities of the audible. We cannot overlook, of course, that the western musical tradition only reluctantly shows an interest in clarifying these

---

8. Cf. Picht, *Kunst und Mythos* (cf. 2), part II.

matters. For it developed so intensely, even obsessively in relation to pitch, notation, linguistic reference and other "Apollonian" organisational criteria that, beyond these, the potency of its "Dionysian" mediality was inevitably doomed to fall behind. It would certainly not be inappropriate to speak of an obliviousness to sound and sound-space extending far into the 19th, perhaps even into the 20th century.[9] This does not suggest a misdirection or a deficit in the obvious sense; on the contrary, we are rather faced with an overwhelming productivity and diversity in the formation of semantic structures which, in a medium that does not for its part allow any distance, indeed create distance — rather like eyes, which assign a position in space to every object.[10] But then, from today's perspective, we must add: the converse of this unleashing of the senses was a rejection of sound-material as such, a notion of the primally acoustic as a derivative reality, an exaggerated emphasis on the force of the sound-space's facticity as such. This power enabled the "abyss of a-semanticity within all sense" (Wellmer) to remain concealed — an abyss that is not simply the counterpart to, but indeed the fundamental condition of sense, i.e. temporal integration. Upon realising this, one can gain an idea of how little the transmitted norms of temporal organisation in music should be taken for granted, and to what degree they have been wrested from the mythical undercurrent of this art, and therefore remain dependent on it.

Although they remain dependent on it, this need not imply an

---

9. This hypothesis would require a more extensive justification than can be offered here, so an encyclopaedic summary will have to suffice: in the 19th century, composers discovered the autonomy of sound; in the late 20th century, music theorists came to realise that sound and timbre are autonomous categories of musical thought, even if they lack representation in the written medium. For a musicological perspective on this cf. Jürgen Maehder, *Klangfarbe als Bauelement des musikalischen Satzes. Zur Kritik des Instrumentationsbegriffes*, (doctoral thesis) Berne 1976.

10. One should realise *what kind* of organisational work in the sense of "overview" comes into play through the introduction of musical notation. In analysing music we treat pitches, intervals, chords and their relationships amongst one another much like objects to be moved around in our visual space. Musical analysis relies on categories that envisage each work — in opposition to the irreversibility of its course — as a synchronously tangible presence. Concerning the opposed necessity to do justice *analytically* to the temporality of sound cf. Ludwig Holtmeier, "Arnold Schönbergs Klavierstück, op. 23, II", in: *Musik & Ästhetik* 12 (1999), pp. 40–52, in particular p. 47 ff.

ontological surrender of music to pure flow, no disappearance of all things concrete in an endless succession of moments taking over from one another; it refers rather to the *presentation* of this disappearance and dissolution. Otherwise, the topos of music's mythical character would be no more than an empty formula. Apollo and Dionysos do not occasion transience as such; they are rather the forces that transfer it into the present, i.e. that enable us to experience it as transience in the first place. Dionysos does of course continue his corrosive, negative work behind Apollo's morphological presence; but he remains vice versa dependent on Apollo, even when all forms and formally constructive effects are essentially drawn into the undertow of an irresistible current. Apollo is the other side of Dionysos, the space of the present that creates meaning; it is he who first discovers the subversive "power of horror" (Picht) and not only provides a counterpoint to the temporal dynamic that pulls the carpet from beneath our feet, but in fact renders it possible at the same time. Within the apparently quite rational talk of coping with and representing time, we still find the tremors of these two old gods' duplicity.

III.

Adorno knew, of course, that the symphonic developmental discourse found in Beethoven's middle period formulates a historical paradigm of temporal organisation, not the absolute truth about the same. Nonetheless, his thoughts on the matter seem to suggest — in a more than fleeting manner — that the composer established in these works *the* experience of time *itself,* and thus *the* measure of all understanding and evaluation of temporal forms in music as such. Any claims to the contrary — such as the critique of ideology found in the commentaries on developmental discourse, the analyses of the extensive form of time,[11] or certain

---

11. Cf. Theodor W. Adorno, *Beethoven. Philosophie der Musik. Fragmente und Texte*, Frankfurt a. M. 1993, p. 74 ff., p. 174 f. (on the intensive form); pp. 134–147, p. 162 ff. (on the extensive form). I have examined both terms more closely in: "Prozessualität und Zuständlichkeit. Konstruktionen musikalischer Zeiterfahrung", in: Otto Kolleritsch (ed.), *Abschied von der Gegenwart. Teleologie und Zuständlichkeit in der Musik*, Vienna/Graz 1998, pp. 180–209.

passages in the book on Mahler — simply lack the daring to offer any more than partial corrections; this normative premise remains essentially unchallenged. Silently, the intensive form thus moves on — or rather up — to the status of a quasi-transhistorical validity, without it having at all shown how and from what perspective this is supposedly possible. "Intensive" here connotes a representation of successivity as a developmental sequence, one that aims not least for an emphatic annulment of time itself: "The introduction of time as an image of transience is the ideal of all music — both of musical experience and musical instruction."[12]

The notion of successivity and development which this reference to an "ideal" implies is drawn on particularly emphatically in the following passage: "Music, as a temporal art, is bound through its very medium to the form of successivity, and is thus as irreversible as time itself. The moment it begins, it is already obliged to continue, to become something new, to develop. This can lend music its transcendence: by the fact of its *becoming* in every moment, it is other than itself: that it should imply something beyond itself is no metaphysical dictate imposed on it, but rather lies in its very nature, *which it cannot compete against.* (...) Since music has existed it has been, among other things, a protest — however powerless — against myth and against the eternal repetition of fate, against death itself. (...) Freedom itself is its immanent pre-requisite. That is its dialectical essence."[13]

There are four weak points here. Firstly, one is taken aback slightly by the idealistic emphasis in both quotations with which,

---

12. Adorno, *Der getreue Korrepetitor. Lehrschriften zur musikalischen Praxis* (*Gesammelte Schriften* vol. 15), Frankfurt a. M. 1997, p. 187. Cf. also *Ästhetische Theorie* (*Gesammelte Schriften* vol. 7), Frankfurt a. M. 1997, p. 48: "By enduring, art protests against death; the short-lived eternity of works is an allegory for a non-apparent eternity. Art is the apparency of that which death cannot reach."
13. Adorno, "Strawinsky. Ein dialektisches Bild", in: *Musikalische Schriften I–III* (*Gesammelte Schriften* vol. 16), Frankfurt a. M. 1997, p. 386 f. (my italics, R.K.). "Sound-space" does not have any *a priori* place here: for Adorno the succession of pitches is the only possible point of departure. Cf. "Kriterien der neuen Musik", op. cit., p. 221: "First of all, music, as a temporal art-form, is dynamic *according to its own material conditions*: just as time is irreversible, anything musical rejects a displacement in time that is indifferent to these." (My italics, R. K.) In his actual theory of musical material, however, this hypothesis does not appear *at all.*

beyond mere rhetorical exaggeration, claims are made for an "ideal" or "essence" of music. Secondly, the understanding of successivity evident here is of a *non-dialectically* contradictory nature. Thirdly, there is consequently a significant imbalance between Adorno's phenomenology and his categorial critique of temporal forms in music. Fourthly — this is a particularly delicate point —, the connection between the ontological and the social level remains unclear. In what follows, I shall take a first look at these problems; a more detailed analysis will have to wait for another occasion.

First point: the validity claimed by Adorno's thoughts on successive time and its "introduction" with reference to Beethoven, or rather with reference to a tradition of composing and of musical thought oriented towards Beethoven, is indeed justified, and can be empirically redeemed. But under no circumstances — in my opinion — does Adorno here formulate the absolute ideal of all music. This view is so hard to reject not only because of such figures as Debussy, Stravinsky and several others, or because temporal experience in music could undoubtedly also be comprehensible from the perspective of our life-span's immanence, which does not require any final negation of the world. The model is questionable rather because its formulation of the *ideal* of temporal representation in music dispenses with any reflection upon this ideal's *premise*. The *Aesthetic Theory* does, of course, contain very dense and impressive passages on the genesis of order in chaos, unity in multiplicity, form in the formless etc. But paradoxically enough, there is no investigation into the causes and origins enabling such formations to ensue. On the subject of time's "earth", Adorno maintains a deathly silence.[14] The intuition that

---

14. Cf. for example *Ästhetische Theorie* (cf. 12), p. 84, p. 145, p. 154 f. Even as late as 1966, in his Darmstadt lecture "Funktion der Farbe in der Musik" (published in: *Darmstadt Dokumente I* [*Musik-Konzepte* Sonderband], Munich 1999, pp. 263–312), he leaves his audience in the dark as to *how* exactly he envisages "sound", insofar as this is the basis for temporal "construction", rather than vice versa. One can generally say that the ontology of purpose is neglected in Adorno's critique of identity, aside from polemical simplifications in the critique of originary philosophy. Origin, however, is not simply that which came first, which is most ancient, subject to compulsive repetition in time; it is also the process of becoming and transpiring, of beginning something new at every moment.

Nietzsche sought to formulate in the names of Apollo and Dionysos ultimately remains foreign to him.

It is for this very reason, however, that the emphasis with which he proclaims—in opposition to Stravinsky—the negation of time or the protest against eternal recurrence and death as the existential duty of music must remain up in the air. Admittedly, this air acknowledges a foundation, i.e. the "fabric" of the musical material, from which it subsequently claims itself to have issued; but Adorno cannot show how and in what sense this is true. In an almost conventionally idealistic manner, his musical philosophy insists on finality and utopian transcendence, as it seeks—in bizarre opposition to its self-identity as dialectical theory—to settle the score with musical time, despite ignoring—or perhaps evading—the object of examination's mythical roots. This demonstrates, at least, the systematic function taken on by Beethoven in these writings in one fundamental respect: the concretion of his works and forms on the one hand, and Adorno's exceptionally rich engagement with them on the other, are *also* substitutes for a temporo-philosophical idea that has not been fully formulated, and whose insufficient theoretical legitimation they do not—through a great diversity of phenomena and a physiognomically close reading of details—so much clarify as rather obscure.[15] Intimacy with music can on occasions resemble a filling that plugs conceptual lacunæ with foreign bodies.

Second point: for Adorno, the self-professed advocate of the ephemeral and transient against the eternal and invariant, time indeed remains, for all its diverse modifications and distinctions, "something" to which music cannot surrender itself, but with which it must rather "come to terms", and whose "empty" flow it must resist, even "pit itself" against.[16] Successivity is initially an empty successivity, a constant sequence of points in the present, a

---

15. Cf. for example *Ästhetische Theorie* (cf. 12), p. 276, on the tendency "towards amorphy" in Beethoven.
16. Cf. Adorno, "Über einige Relationen zwischen Musik und Malerei", in: *Musikalische Schriften I–III* (*Gesammelte Schriften* vol. 16), Frankfurt a. M. 1997, p. 628. In another passage he even speaks of a power "that would *annul* time". (*Einleitung in die Musiksoziologie. Zwölf theoretische Vorlesungen* [*Gesammelte Schriften* vol. 14], Frankfurt a. M. 1997, p. 230; my italics, R. K.)

homogeneous divisional horizon. This, however, indicates less a formal fact than an abstracted force, the scheme of an inexorable nullity which music must "pit itself" against: temporal art is thus defined by an *a priori* resistance to the "empty course of time, the senseless flow of life."[17] When Adorno speaks in this context of "boredom",[18] and of the "fear ... of the linear flow of time",[19] he does not simply mean a negative condition of the soul, but rather an ontological fact, even if he naturally terms it differently. Boredom is the central sign or symptom, as it were the identity tag of the primacy of terrestrial time over that of individual life. It reminds us that our life is embedded in terrestrial time, and dominated by it to a degree inaccessibly far beyond any finite intentions, plans and projects. It is therefore clear: Adorno's reference to the introduction of time ultimately formulates a theological imperative to rid the world of all boredom; the supremacy of terrestrial time over our lives does not, indeed cannot be allowed to have the last word. It is this unattainable goal, this impossible wish that it is music's task to assist in expressing.

To define successivity in this fashion, i.e. with reference to a continuous sequence of points in the present, is therefore insufficient. Successivity rather implies — by necessity — irreversibility, i.e. transience. One could never say of a homogeneous parameter that for its duration it is "'long'-winded, and faces humans as a reified, estranged, threatening object." One can speak reasonably of such a threat only with reference to both the asymmetrical temporality of existence *and* the modern capitalist dichotomy between abstract and living, measured and experienced time. Adorno occasionally remarks on the latter of these two aspects, but entirely

---

17. Adorno/Horkheimer, *Dialektik der Aufklärung* (*Gesammelte Schriften* vol. 3), Frankfurt a. M. 1997, p. 312 (appendix: "Das Schema der Massenkultur").
18. "While the primitive consciousness desires for music to alleviate times of boredom, the liberated consciousness comes home to this goal once it has freed itself from it, and in so doing also cured music of its boredom. The introduction of time as an image of transience is the ideal of all music — both of musical experience and musical instruction." (Adorno, *Der getreue Korrepetitor* [cf. 12], p. 187.)
19. Adorno, "Zweite Nachtmusik", in: *Musikalische Schriften V* (*Gesammelte Schriften* vol. 18), Frankfurt a. M. 1997, p. 51. The following quotation is taken from the same page.

ignores the former; he leaves Heidegger's question "Why do we say that time *passes*, but not with *equal* emphasis that time arises?"[20] unposed. This does not, however, prevent him from, in effect, appropriating Heidegger's own answer—namely that our "elusive" knowledge of the end implicitly binds together our understanding of a) transience and b) the constant sequence of moments in the present—by stating that "in the works of Beethoven, the profane composer, empty, estranged time pushes lethally forwards against the subject."[21]

But he does not simply effect a *de facto* appropriation—he avoids a genuine engagement with the problem. *What is lacking in Adorno's writings is a theory of temporal dimensionality*—both of existence and music—which could enable us to articulate adequately the question as to the possibility of freedom in the face of death, whether in agreement with Heidegger, in opposition to Heidegger, or in agreement with *and* in opposition to Heidegger. By confining himself to a "vulgar" understanding of time as successivity, he brings about his own entanglement in an irresolvable contradiction.

For Adorno, time is firstly a form of abstract negativity, the senseless flow of life, a void that pushes lethally forwards; but secondly, it is also a medium of non-identity, openness and otherness *par excellence*. What is the connection between the two? In the passage on Stravinsky cited above, he resorts to an idea that is rather unusual for him: an *ontological deduction* of the second from the first, of intensive time from empirical pitch-sequences as music's constitutional norm. As sonic events cannot but occur successively, the only option is to compose according to processual negativity and developmental history,[22] be it in the most

---

20. Martin Heidegger, *Sein und Zeit*, Tübingen[15] 1979, p. 425.
21. Adorno, "Kriterien der neuen Musik" (cf. 12); p. 222. Time can only be "empty", however, as a homogeneous parameter. Irreversability and fatality are themselves qualitative *and asymmetrical* classifications. To speak of irreversible time as empty or abstract is to ignore existential temporality *a priori*. Cf. aphorisms nos. 49, 105 and 106 in *Minima Moralia*.
22. On "development" and the "irreversibility of time" cf. Adorno, *Beethoven* (cf. 11), p. 106 f.

deformed, shrunken or fragmented of forms.[23] The final transcendence of space thus derives directly from the order of successivity, without the distinction between time as "mere unleashed transience"[24] and time as the horizon of freedom and difference being accorded any great significance, and indeed without any mediation — in whatever form — between this idea and the present, the immediate moment, to say nothing of compositional issues. How, under such circumstances, is the "introduction of time" at all possible? Without any reference to the present, irreversibility as a medium of freedom cannot even be conceived, let alone realised in music. It would be absurd to suppose that Adorno did not "know" this; he reclaims the notion of existence in and of itself on multiple occasions as an unrelinquishable outpost against universal tendencies towards temporalisation.[25] Yet, in situations calling for specific mediation, he seeks refuge in generalised dichotomies or declarations — where he presents freedom as a consequence of irreversibility, he says nothing of presence; and where he speaks of presence, any notion of irreversibility as a condition for freedom is anathema. In both cases, the thought-process comes to an abrupt halt, and the relationship between the two aspects remains

---

23. "One could easily choose to interpret this as a form of thinking that revolves around musical invariance, whether one rejoices at the notion of extrapolating an entire ontology from the sheer flow of time, or polemically — eager to deny the validity even of these final invariants — suspects the gravity of that which has already proven fruitless to be at the root of this claim. (...) Any zealous attempts to deny the structural conditions imposed on music by its own *inexorable* temporality are futile." (Adorno, "Form in der neuen Musik", in: *Musikalische Schriften I–III* [cf. 13], p. 615; my italics, R. K.)

24. Adorno, "Strawinsky. Ein dialektisches Bild" (cf. 13), p. 388.

25. Cf. Adorno, *Philosophie der neuen Musik* (*Gesammelte Schriften* vol. 12), Frankfurt a. M. 1997, p. 58: "Only for as long as (...) an autonomous musical thing-in-itself is — in the Kantian sense — imposed upon it, as it were, can music invole that which keeps the empty force of time at bay." Cf. op. cit., p. 92: The concept of time "is justified in its existence only through its conquest of the unresolved, conflicting elements assailing it within itself. Without the priority of such an objectively existent musical entity to test its strength against, it becomes a meaningless contrivance and is swamped by an undifferentiated continuum." Cf. also "Kriterien der neuen Musik" (cf. 13), p. 217: "If music is truly the history of a theme, then only because anything that has a history already 'is' in and of itself, as the literal sense of 'theme', i.e. something which is 'posited' intends."

a mystery. The categorial fixation upon successivity and development precludes the possibility of any notion of "ecstatic" temporality from the outset.[26]

Third point: in failing to meet this demand, Adorno prevents his thoughts on forms of musical time from being unified within a coherent terminological construction. In phenomenological terms, the decay of time — with regard to both "Romantic and genuinely new music"[27] — is defined and developed unambiguously as the form in which the subject appears, and with which it — as a subject — must "cope". Adorno's categorial approach, however, works on the assumption that the object of decay can be preserved through and beyond the course of its decay, i.e. that it ultimately cannot, indeed must not — despite all claims to the contrary — constitute anything finite which grows and passes within history. He describes the undermining and ultimately the suspension of the classical temporal consciousness, i.e. the transformation of development and processuality into comparitively "static" configurations, as the outstanding structural hallmark — whatever differences of detail there may be — of *all* music since Beethoven.

In Schubert's music it is the corrosion of developmental processes through repetition, expressive association and episodic fields; in Wagner's it is the overgrowth of the evolutionary principle, which strives to reach out towards an open future through a stationary, "mythical" system that paralyses this attempt and changes it into a synchronous order of something eternally the same, yet also boundless; with Mahler it is the ambivalence

---

26. The relationship between successive time and dialectics would be a topic of its own. Is a dialectical understanding of time restricted to time as succession *and* its negation? Does dialectic necessarily imply a logification of time? And is *homogeneous* succession the *conditio sine qua non* for precisely this, namely the identity-scheme that enables time to be understood *and negated* in logical forms as a process, i.e. as a confluence of divergent modes and as a historical dynamic? The inadequacy of this approach becomes clear, for example when Adorno writes that the flow of time becomes such "only by remembering that (...) which *has already been* and which *contradicts* its flow." ("Form in der neuen Musik", in: *Musikalische Schriften I–III* [cf. 13], p. 615 [my italics, R. K.].) How, in all seriousness, can the fact that we *are* our past contradict the irreversibility of time's course? Such claims as this have always disregarded the "*a priori*" of the temporal dimensionalisation of the "immediate".
27. Adorno, *Philosophie der neuen Musik* (cf. 25), p. 181.

between an almost overflowing, epic outpouring of richness and the counter-elements of a — albeit broken — historicity of the flow of musical time; with Debussy it is the transferral of temporal progress into a medium serving the exposition of simultaneous sonic effects and spaces; in Stravinsky's music it is a "cubism" of transitionless, as it were anorganic layerings of heterogeneous blocks; in Schönberg's it is the reflected deferral of subjective historicity through a universalisation of motivic-thematic methods. In short, the decay of time as the "being" of the "subject" in favour of a force that goes unreachably far ahead of this subject, and which justifies it to the same degree that it rules and penetrates it, characterises at an analytical level — according to Adorno — almost all relevant compositional forms of the 19th and 20th centuries.

Adorno does not, however, draw the full categorial conclusion from this. He rather tries — as his critiques of Wagner and Stravinsky, but also of Schönberg's dodecaphony and serialism show — to establish a normative opposition: the opposition between an *immanently reflected* dissociation and reification of temporality that remains derived — however critically it may present this derivation — from a subjective interiority that surrenders itself to the tones, in Hegel's sense, and a *now merely external* "retreat of time into space",[28] where the "things themselves", the physical bodies, the world's horizons as such are made to sound, albeit without a throwback to mediatory self-presence being at all possible, let alone explicitly desired.

But behind this normative polarisation of intensive and extensive spatialisation stands the ontologisation of successivity mentioned above, whose absurdity becomes particularly apparent in the critique of Stravinsky. Adorno speaks there of the "temporal dialectic" as the "inapparency of music", which Stravinsky replaces with the "apparency of atemporal proportions." He claims that Stravinsky "manipulates the course of music *as if* temporal successivity could directly be constrained to form a temporal adjacency; *as if* motives were interchangeable cubes and surfaces."[29] This hypothesis is afflicted by a fundamentalism to which it is

---

28. ibid., p. 173.
29. Adorno, "Kriterien der neuen Musik" (cf. 13), p. 222.

oblivious: as motives and rhythms can "in reality" simply not be structured like cubes or surfaces (and who would deny this?), one should no more be allowed to ascribe this capacity to them in the context of "apparency". As it is beyond doubt that no composer in the world can *literally* accommodate the forces and potentialities of musical material within an order of spatial extension, even the *fiction*, or perhaps the *play* of a restriction or elimination of temporal irreversibility in music tends to be discarded as an "anti-realist manipulation". This argument feeds off a form of second-degree theory of representation. It would even lead to Adorno being branded as the Lukács of musical philosophy if his capacity as a phenomenologist did not have the rare merit of dissolving the categorial fixities of its own critique, and thus allowing the multiplicity and diversity of that which can be historically experienced *in musicis* to triumph over premature evaluations and clarifications. For it is not only in relation to Stravinsky that the normative contrasting of immanent temporal suspension and external spatialisation in fact proves less sophisticated than the phenomenon which it claims to understand and even to define.

Fourth point: one could, of course, level the charge of "ontologisation" — in the sense encountered in Critical Theory — at these deliberations: are we not ignoring the socio-critical directionality of Adorno's reflections in favour of pure philosophical speculation? Am I not, under the pretext of being obliged to consider "deeper" matters than capitalism, myself merely paying tribute to its rulership? Am I myself not in fact guilty of subservience to this prosthetic god and to the law of social amnesia that constitutes him by not shedding light on the possibilities of changing it, instead pursuing the aporiai of this change's intra-musical consequences? This objection comes too hastily, however, as good as it may sound. Social theory should by no means be excluded from aesthetic debates. But it is rather unclear to me how exactly it comes into them, or perhaps where it is located there, and what meaning, what implications it has in the matter. In any case, there is — after all that has been said — ample reason to assume that this inclarity is not simply to be attributed to gaps in my understanding of Adorno, but in fact also to a problem-area that is symptomatic of Adorno's own thinking.

The fact remains that Adorno himself undermines the *differentiation* between socio-theoretical and ontological terms whose necessity *in musicis* is implied in his work.[30] He thus not only distinguishes insufficiently between the ontological ambivalence of time resulting from the *irrevocable* difference between its modes and modalities on the one hand, and the social irreconcialition resulting from the *as yet unresolved* antagonism of the capitalist system on the other; he even equates the two, inasmuch as for him the non-identity of temporal modes implicitly remains devoted to the task of critically dissecting the untruthful "omnipresence of the equivalential relation"[31] (as well as the dominance of successive over dimensionalised time bound up in it) and bringing to light a reconciliatory "image of the end of transience" *ex negativo* through the depiction of irreconciled circumstances. It is difficult to see how such a construction of reconcialition is supposed to prevent, by ignoring the differences between temporal modes, not envisioning or yearning for a true, i.e. lasting—and conclusive, thus timeless—present. It is not by any means my intention to question Adorno's social analyses of the music of Beethoven, Wagner, Schönberg etc. as such. I simply refute the claim that the impossibility of a constant resolution of the tension between the temporal forms in these musics can be unequivocally attributed to the fact that "in actual society, the harmony of individual and collective interests taught by liberalism failed."[32]

---

30. In a letter to Horkheimer from the 12.6.1941, Adorno at least concedes, with relation to music, that "there is something to the question of time as one *sui generis*". (Max Horkheimer, *Briefwechsel 1941–1948* [*Gesammelte Schriften* vol.17], Frankfurt a. M. 1996, p. 60) He does not himself draw any conclusions from this; but he paves the way for them, i.e. he implies between the lines that a sociological condensation of the problem is not sufficient of itself. Significantly, references to society are generally withheld in precisely those passages dealing with a musical negation of time or with musical processuality. (Cf. the passages cited in footnotes 23 and 25). Conversely, one does not find a single mention of the temporal problem in Adorno's countless statements on the representation of social contradictions in musical forms. Whatever there may be to say on this in detail, it is hard to dismiss the assumption that we are dealing here with the scar of a concealed problem.
31. Adorno, *Einleitung in die Musiksoziologie* (cf. 16), p. 228.
32. Adorno, "Form in der neuen Musik", in: *Musikalische Schriften I–III* (cf. 13), p. 611. The fact that our temporal understanding is "socially mediated" does not eliminate the question as to what temporal position society for its part occupies.

In Adorno's thinking, music's ability to point beyond the ideology of social circumstances remains tied to the originarily metaphysical capacity for "eradicating" time as such and attaining some sort of freedom from its governance. Conceiving of the composed work in itself as the critique of social processes can only be achieved at the price of an act of force: Adorno transposes the twofold ontological difference of time (that between its modes and that between the two temporal rows) to a utopian reconciliatory horizon; from this point it appears, as it were under the patronage of irreconciled negativity, as "not yet resolved, but principally resolvable" — and this can in turn mark the vanishing point of the work's capacity for immanent resistance against the present conditions. As much as this philosophy of music might insist on the impaired nature of compositional structures and forms, it equally yearns with all its heart to escape them one day just for a moment, perhaps even once and for all. It would admittedly be misguided to tie Adorno's theory to a theological enthusiasm of this kind, or even to focus it in some relation to it. But, inasmuch as he arbitrarily passes over the horizon of our experiential time-span, or indeed — and this amounts to the same thing — "hopelessly" confuses existential and metaphysical experience, one shall have to bid farewell to his conception of a philosophy of music.

IV.

A musical work is not a final object. If it were, it would have to be definable as something beyond its own medial forms of representation. It only exists in these forms, however, or rather in their interplay; it cannot assign or subordinate them as aspects of itself. The work is not the transcendence of its representational spaces, and these spaces are for their part not media of external appearance, in which the inner spiritual content of a work is expressed purely through the senses; they are rather the ways in which the work exists as a whole, in which it is real. In music, this existence is split into the twofold entity of the written score and the sounding event. The musical work is the dynamically unfolding relationship between text and performance, notation and sound-experience. Any attempt to gain clarity concerning the temporality of music in its various aspects must by necessity incorporate an analysis of the temporal interplay of its representational media. This also serves to clarify what possibilities of differentiation the work-concept included in its originary form. It is crassly inadequate to treat this category like some historical fossil that no longer has any meaning, or to act as if one is dealing with a monster, one that by default attacks the diversity and vitality of our unique experiences by having nothing but invariance and identity to offer.

As a score, music is existent and available as an object; as a performance, however, it is born and disappears differently, uniquely and suddenly each time. The introduction of its temporal strains in the score-object can be interpreted as a revolt against time in the sense of mere successivity, but equally as its fulfilment and perfection. At the same time, the sound-event has the status of an internal correction or even subversion of the work-character, in that as the work appears through it as if it had only now come into existence, had only now been born, and equally: as it can only be this one time, then never again. Concerts are, as it were, the rehearsal of an "hour" that has never before existed and shall never exist anymore, *and* which, rather than exhausting itself in the plain transience of successivity as such, reclaims a presence of meaning that can precisely not be deduced from the scheme of sequence, from such notions as before and after. As the hour of meaning, music has always been what supposedly only *performance art* succeeded in being: a unique, all-consuming act of fulfilment that resists both an immaculate repetition and a levelling-out through a surfeit of richness. To bring music thus into position as a singular event — one is tempted to say: as a compression of life itself — against the music industry, dominated as it is by technical reproduction, does not mean giving a new lease of life to the old ideology which postulates that music can have no meaning or reality outside of the performance, to which the score is purely and instrumentally subordinate. There is no cause for anti-textuality: the genuinely sounding tone-constellation does not represent the finished work any more than do the possibilities of genuine sounding "foreshadowed" in the score. Without doubt the aesthetic of suddenness is nowhere more at home than in music, in the sonic stab or blow that overpowers me or into which I am drawn, and which as it were condenses an existence from birth until death into a single moment. Nonetheless, the specific freedom of this event would be impossible were it not for its embedding in a structure of basal repeatability that precedes it in the written medium.

Gadamer, the philosopher of play, has quite rightly insisted that performance represents "the work itself"[33] and not any subordinate mode of it. The work's place is in the world within which it presents itself, i.e. it is substantially present in the musical performance, in the processes of playing and listening, not simply as the sensual exterior of an intellective sensory whole. One is exposed to it and involved in it; it is neither a matter of viewing an object from the outside nor of "empathising" with the enigmatic project of a soul that is "entirely other". Nonetheless, for all personal involvement, for all ecstasy *in actu*, the musical work is not expended in the phenomenality of its sonic reality. The living tone of performance could not be without the lifeless muteness of the score's symbols. These do not merely serve the technical realisation of a performance as a tablature or set of instructions; they are always also the bearers of sensory relations which cannot, or at least not immediately, be heard. Their medial potency is revealed through the fact that they take into account *now* — against the overpowering sensual presence of sound — the wealth of other, i.e. past and possible future realisations of the work, with the distance they offer. The score allows us to perceive the work as something that lies or stands beyond all fixed attempts to interpret it. In this sense, we can say — to cite Gadamer — that works are "only ever genuinely present when we return to them."[34] The facticity of prior possibilities is as much their own as the subversive experience that consumes itself in the moment. The explosion which the performance appears as can only be carried out and understood in its singularity because there already exists an open field of play which

---

33. Hans-Georg Gadamer, *Hermeneutik I. Wahrheit und Methode. Grundzüge einer philosophischen Hermeneutik* (*Gesammelte Werke* vol. 1), Tübingen 1999, p. 121.
34. Gadamer, *Text und Interpretation*, in: *Hermeneutik II. Wahrheit und Methode. Ergänzungen und Register* (*Gesammelte Werke* vol. 2), Tübingen 1999, p. 351.

designs the work each time as the epitome of that which can be returned to, only *thus* providing the fireworks of *performance**[35] with the stage upon which to articulate its elusive sense.

Admittedly, it seems difficult to establish a connection between the two medial poles without suppressing their differences, or perhaps to deal with the tension between them without fixating them upon themselves. Frequently, music is viewed strictly dualistically *either* as a text *or* an event. Both tendencies here see themselves in opposition to a music industry governed by the principles of reproductive technology. The one, the script-fixated, tends to edit the event out of the work, believing that it "objectively" commands a presence of meaning that is independent from the temporality of sound; the other, however, the sound-fixated tendency, reduces music to its temporal consumption, recognising in the *a priori* of the work's reproducibility only a rigid scheme to be opposed by subverting it through the unique, the vitally transient.

The preference for music as text, as cultivated and developed at a high level by Rudolf Kolisch, derives its justification from particular aspects of industrialised musical life — such as the increasing disappearance of the text as an independent bearer of meaning in favour of its empiricist functionalisation, the reduction of notational symbols to mere means of *performance**, as well as the (in part) undoubtedly regressive consequences of such aspects for musical training and teaching. The gain in analytical culture occasioned by Kolisch's "Zurück zum Text" need hardly be pointed out. At the same time, however, its price is no less than a denial of music's constitutive temporality. For Kolisch, the performance is ultimately but a realisation of the meaning contained in the text, i.e. the score, and is in this sense emphatically superfluous as a requisite for its genuine consumption.[36] He argues his case as if musical analyses were in a position to reveal a work's meaning as

---

35. Translator's note: the asterisk indicates that this word is in English in the original text.
36. Cf. in particular Rudolf Kolisch, *Zur Theorie der Aufführung. Ein Gespräch mit Berthold Türcke* (*Musik-Konzepte* 29/30), Munich 1983, esp. pp. 9–16. Cf. also Heinz-Klaus-Metzger, *Restitutio Musicae. Zur Intervention Kolischs*, in: *Beethoven. Das Problem der Interpretation* (*Musik-Konzepte* 8), Munich 1979, pp. 54–69.

"objectively determinable", without the necessity of becoming an event within a unique, unrepeatable time-span. But this is both idealistic hubris and obstinacy.

The self-evidence of the difference between sonic reality and the musical work, as well as the resulting consequences for any study of the score that deserves the name, justify neither an ontological reduction of the work to the notated text nor a culturo-critical trivialisation of the ban on graven images, which claims that empirical musical life does such an injustice to the works that, for the sake of upholding the truth, one should read scores *instead of* attending or holding concerts—or, worse still, indulging in recordings. This idealisation of the text that devalues the sound-event is the triumph of a positivism that mistakes itself for critical metaphysics.[37] Against this phantasm of ideality, Picht's dictum remains unadulteratedly valid: "music is an event, or it is not music."[38]

But no more is it recommendable to play off ephemerality against longevity and to demand or celebrate a "transformation of the work into action, into an event"[39]—even if there is an element of truth in this: for this reclaims an approach to time that

---

37. The interplay of idealism and positivism is characteristic of Kolisch's theory as a whole. One aspect is the imperative of a functional realisation of musical sense, which "translates without exception" the results of score-analysis "into correlates of performance practice" (Metzger, "Zur Beethoven-Interpretation", in: *Beethoven*, op. cit., p. 6) At the same time, the finite performance is seen as obviously falling short of the work's ineffability: "*One* performance is insufficient. (...) What can be gained by hearing it [the work] only *once*?" (Kolisch/Türcke, *Gespräch*, in: *Zur Theorie der Aufführung*, op. cit., p. 12 & 16.)

38. Picht, *Grundlinien einer Philosophie der Musik* (footnote 2), p. 424. It would constitute a study in its own right to examine the common traits and differences between Kolisch and Adorno. Both intended to write a theory of performance together, but significantly did not. Kolisch's idealisation of the score and the consequent devaluation of the sounding result were in part supported by Adorno; but for his whole life he also revered Wilhelm Furtwängler, the conductor of the mythical musical event *par excellence*, to the same degree that he battled, on the other hand, against Toscanini (who was—and still is—much respected among Kolisch's students) as the representative of a merely technically-oriented devotion to the text. This contradiction remains a noteworthy one.

39. Dieter Mersch, "Ereignis und Aura. Zur Dialektik von ästhetischem und kulturellem Gedächtnis", in: *Musik & Ästhetik 3* (1997), p. 23.

opposes the dictates of reproductive technology, which relies utterly on perfect reference, unlimited repeatability and a neutralisation through excess. In a culture characterised by turning away and forgetting, it is a legitimate concern to render points and moments of genuine intensity possible. For this reason, however, merely setting the work of art against *performance art**, metaphysical sense against ephemeral action, imperial monument against contingent consumption, remains a crudely abstract categorisation, and is itself afflicted by the loss of history it attacks. If anything allows the work-idea to outlive its ideology, then it is its fundamental imperative not to surrender the temporal art to time, but rather to come to terms with time and represent it; not to practise a mystification of mere fulfilment, but rather to find a means of expressing the interplay of the moment, memory and the trajectory of change. If one is serious about the critique of fetishes, one should not—be it compositionally or aesthetically—lightheartedly squander this potential. The idealisation of the score and the celebration of the *sound** are equally opposed to the historicity of the work. The upshot of this is not, however, an apologia for the substantialist work-idea, but rather a plea for its media-aesthetic differentiation.

Seen (or heard) in this light, some tendencies encountered in "aleatory"[40] composition and indeterminate music, which where in their heyday received primarily as a dissolution of the work-idea, would have to be viewed rather as a complex modification thereof: firstly in the sense that, for example in Boulez' Third Piano Sonata, a kind of music was composed that no recording could "faithfully" reproduce, as it was based on forms which depend on "chance", i.e. on the contingency of the performance situation and the interpretative decisions that must be made anew each time; and secondly in the sense of a further refinement of our

---

40. I realise that I am operating with a pre-scientific notion of the aleatory by including in this category all forms that emancipate the media of representation from the work-idea, or rather enable the work-idea to be changed into its representational media. So far, however, there has not been any more scientific notion. Cf. Winrich Hopp, *"Kurzwellen" von Karlheinz Stockhausen. Konzeption und musikalische Poiesis*, Mainz 1998.

notion of musical time that *expressly* encompasses the web of relations between its spaces of medial representation, i.e. the individual constellations of script and sound, score and performance, of fixed structure, open possibilities and the unrepeatable event. Certainly, aleatory composition definitively oversteps the work's boundaries as a monad and a principle of reflexive internality; it shows that it continues to come into existence — and be at stake — anew, and that it cannot exist independently of its medial representations, actions and interpretations. At the same time, its tendency towards repeatability does not automatically contradict the historical and medial dynamic of art; the polarity of the work-idea as such is hardly abandoned alone through an emphatic recognition of contingency. On the contrary, it could be shown that precisely the outstanding examples of a "music of chance" renew the fundamental tension between the facticity of the basally repeatable and the singularity of productive interpretations — i.e. the entire play of the moment, change and memory —, each time with their own specific emphases, even to the extent that the work, as a constant field of relations between "all" aspects, only comes about afterwards, *a posteriori*, in the wake of particular performance practices and their scientific analysis. One way or another or yet another: the notion of the work is as inevitable as its requirement that music should not be surrendered to the force of time, but should rather open a space in relation to it, a freedom to gain access to it: *the musical work is and fulfils an immanent transcendence.*[41]

V.

The idea of a freedom *from* time in contemporary philosophy is espoused most decidedly by Michael Theunissen. Theunissen is concerned — especially in confrontation with Heidegger — with rendering possibilities of resistance against, as he terms it, the "rule of time" — i.e. against the negativity of time that governs our lives — philosophically conceivable. I cannot deal closely with this

---

41. I had originally intended to develop this idea of an immanent transcendence of freedom *to* time in a section on Gadamer, and then to confront it with Theunissen's outline of a freedom *from* time. This plan had to be abandoned for reasons of space.

approach here; what is interesting, however, is that Theunissen supports it not least with reference to Adorno. For him, Adorno is not simply a critic of metaphysical ideologies of eternity who uncovers the "eternally invariant", i.e. the principles that level out and deny time; he is also the one whose critique of this "unreal eternity" of metaphysics "(is meant to) clear a space for the real. It thus simultaneously turns", writes Theunissen, "against the thinking that seeks to emancipate itself from metaphysics in opposing above all the two primary tendencies of this school of thought: the universalisation and the affirmation of time."[42]

Now Adorno did not recognisably engage with Heidegger's philosophy of time in any work; but philology is not what is needed here. Theunissen's interpretative forcefulness rather brings to light an aspect of Adorno's thinking that leads a shadow-life in his genuinely philosophical works and only finds comparatively open expression — if not any substantial legitimation — in his writings on music. One could put it like this: Adorno stands in a similar — albeit not identical — opposition to Heidegger's "universalisation and affirmation of time" as Theunissen considers necessary in the sense of a critical reading of modern existence. Adorno's polemic against Heidegger's conception of death may miss the point in several respects, but in one aspect its philosophical sense can hardly be refuted: in its rejection of an absolutised finitude of existential ontology and thus — indirectly — also of an understanding of time as a universal *a priori* beyond which we cannot thinkingly see or experience any form of truth whatsoever. Whatever may be meant by the enigmatic reflections on a "temporal core of truth," it certainly has nothing to do with time as an originary medium of, as it were, a-transcendental universality, which is at once "the condition for the possibility of everything we can say yes to." (40) In Heidegger's violent rejection of any dialectic of boundaries, in his attempt to contemplate in the manner of an atheistic Luther — i.e. as if there were, as if there could be only

---

42. Theunissen, *Negative Theologie der Zeit* (cf. 5), p. 41. The page-numbers of the next four citations are supplied in the text. On the "temporal core of truth" cf. Adorno, *Zur Metakritik der Erkenntnistheorie. Studien über Husserl und die phänomenologischen Antinomien* (*Gesammelte Schriften* vol. 5), Frankfurt a. M. 1971, p. 141.

one side to the boundary, as if our life were fenced in by a black wall beyond which "nothing is" —, his dialectical critics see an ideologisation of finitude at work that rules out significant possibilities for human freedom, and also his capacity for suffering at the negativity of time, i.e. the transience of life and its dynamic of loss.

Theunissen's emphasis on a suffering at time[43] is not an *ad hoc* return to Platonic metaphysics. He does not deny that time is a fundamental condition for our self-realisation and for the sense in life attainable for each one of us; he simply emphasises that it does not as such, i.e. as an "ontological" web of ecstasies, yet possess an "ontical" sense, and *therefore* necessarily becomes conspicuous, becomes the "object" of reflexive processes as well as ailments of the soul, to the same extent that the meaning of our life — and that of our social self-perception — is emptied, dissociated, and dissolved. The call to "cross out Heidegger's affirmation of time entirely" (45) is therefore less a plea for a mystical turning away from the world than an overstated reminder that time is more than the "being of the subject" (Hegel), that even from the perspective of a successful life it remains a foreign might that resists all attempts to appropriate or integrate it. However — and this addition is indispensable —: every subjectively inaccessible otherness of time is nonetheless of a kind that enables a presence, or present*ness*, within which time can, as it were, be turned against itself, where one can say *no* with and through its originary possibilities. Freedom from time is not a direct leap into transcendence, but rather the "result of the (im)potent attempt to play off time against time," (58) to handle it, so to speak, like a tool for constructing a presence beyond itself.

In a freedom from time, Theunisssen sees the implication, indeed the embodiment of an emphatic contentment; and one form concerned with the representation of this contentment, i.e.

---

43. Translator's note: the German phrase *Leiden an Zeit* poses the problem that, in everyday language, *leiden an* means to suffer *from*, as with an illness; clearly this would be inappropriate here. To speak of suffering *under* would come rather closer, but is still unsatisfactory, insofar as its German correlate is *leiden unter*. The slightly unwieldy *suffering at* has thus been chosen for the sake of deeper faithfulness.

our striving towards it and its *impaired* realisation, is art. He writes on art: "The utopian in all art — to the extent that it is internal to it and compatible with the autonomy of each work — is based on just such a materialisation of our striving for freedom from time. Social utopias can only avoid destroying the autonomy of each work of art if they are mediated through the objectivation of the subjective will to freedom, which — as the existence of a freedom from time — transforms the image into a symbol of successful life." (288) Theunissen here utters the secret of Adorno's philosophy of music which it itself does not dare to fully envisage: without the ontological and existential premises that it silently posits, the social critique of a work of art could not be what it is. Not only can the forms of musical time be understood as depicting social contradictions; this depiction itself only becomes possible in the light of a utopian freedom from time that cannot be deduced from the facticities of social structure. Like Adorno, Theunissen considers it possible, indeed necessary, to legitimate a utopian perspective through the autonomy of a work of art that sets itself apart from the rest of the world. This perspective is not imposed on the work from the outside, either as a political or a philosophical foreign body: it rather follows from its own irrevocable temporal and temporally-resistant constitution. This constitution is irrevocable to the extent that freedom from time can, under the conditions of our life, only take on an impaired reality — but an impaired form at least, and thoroughly so. It is the work of art that assists this impairment in gaining expression.

To speak of time in this context as "irrevocable" assumes, admittedly, that the speculative figure of the "end of art" is no longer systematically effective. The utopia of the autonomous work of art cannot, it seems to me, be an indication or an anticipation of possibilities principally accessible to historical practical methods that are "only" waiting to be caught up with — at whatever point that might be — and seized. The work of art is not a higher provisional form of meaning that shall one day be superseded by an ultimate fulfilment of sense. It is precisely the existential legitimation of its utopian experiential dimension that is confronted with a reconciliatory philosophy's conclusional scheme that renders art emphatically "superfluous" by fulfilling its promise and accomplishing its truth.⁴⁴ But the question is: what does timelessness *in* time actually mean? And what is the dialectic of the boundary?

Albrecht Wellmer reveals the mutual incompatibility of aesthetic reconciliatory finalism and the structure of the finite artistic experience in a particularly poignant fashion.⁴⁵ One should note three aspects of his reflections.

Firstly, finitude is either fallen short of or simply bypassed if the reconciliatory discourse is already conceived in such a form that fulfilling the aesthetic promise of happiness must by necessity occasion the end of art, its demise in a reconciled constitution of the world. As long as one operates within the framework of such a model, neither the specificity of aesthetic experience nor the particularity of the aesthetic object can be adequately expressed, even where one harbours the opposite intention and begins by deconstructing the reconciliatory principle itself. Any phenomenology of the works that deserves the name must, if necessary, remain suppressed in favour of purely philosophical speculations (on the apperception of truth, the possibility of a good life, the purpose of history etc.) which ultimately instrumentalise art.

Secondly, Wellmer turns Heidegger's polemical figure of world and earth against the historico-philosophical yardstick of Adorno's

---

44. My question to Theunissen would be: how can one say of the "otherness of time" that it renders "the present-eternity... so co-present that I now understand what has always been meant by the *other*, and even what it could one day truly be" (*Negative Theologie der Zeit* [cf. 5], p. 295), yet at the same time avoid the consequences we have observed in Adorno's philosophy of reconciliation? Even if I believe that a "joyous yearning" which is, as Goethe expresses it, "in the end desirous of the light" is a constitutive part of the artistic experience, do I then require a "present-eternity" that "has always" waited for me to "one day" be struck by it? Is it a matter of a "real" transcendence *in actu*, or not rather the *presenceable* "striving" after it? Is the due realisation of possibility, the fulfilment of a wish the measure *or* is it rather the possibility, the wish itself in its unstable presence and its affectation by the negativity of historical reality?
45. Cf. Albrecht Wellmer, "Das Versprechen des Glücks und warum es gebrochen werden muß", in: Otto Kolleritsch (ed.), *Das gebrochene Glücksversprechen. Zur Dialektik des Harmonischen in der Musik* (Studien zur Wertungsforschung vol. 33), Vienna/Graz 1998, pp. 10–37. Cf. also the earlier essay "Adorno, die Moderne und das Erhabene", in: *Endspiele: Die unversöhnliche Moderne. Essays und Vorträge*, Frankfurt a. M. 1993, pp. 178–203, esp. p. 193 ff. As far as the recourse to Heidegger is concerned, I refer to an as yet unpublished manuscript by Wellmer written in 1996: "Über Musik und Sprache — Musik verstehen".

aesthetics. Heidegger argues: in setting up a world, the work of art creates the earth; but this causes it to be split by an originary rift that can by necessity not be closed up, i.e. "reconciled", as it represents that which conditions the work itself. Wellmer infers: if this is the case, then there can no longer be any possibility of interpreting the work according to the stipulation of ultimate foundations of knowledge or life, ultimate goals of history and ultimate solutions and salvations. If every complex of meaning that can be uncovered in unfolding form in the work ("world") for its part remains tied to the element of self-closure, the asemantic material basis — and abyss — of meaning which every interpretation rebounds off ("earth"), then the possibility of envisioning art as a medium and a premonition of a not-yet-existent truth has aleady been lost to such a degree that no further replacement can exist that would *not* be compelled to subjugate art to a scheme external to it.

Thirdly, Wellmer casts doubt on the validity of the aesthetic reconciliatory notion not only in the historico-philosophical sense, but also in relation to its conceivability and thus *de facto* to its existential relevance: "Is the promise of a 'non-illusorily present contentment', a non-illusory presence of the absolute, not a strictly speaking inconceivable, an impossible, an incomprehensible promise, ultimately indistinguishable from the promise of Nirvana...? The traits of finitude, of transience, of non-presence ... are so deeply embedded in the contentment which we alone can know — and also the contentment of aesthetic experience — that we literally no longer know what we are talking about if we attempt to envisage it without these traces of the finite. (...) How can a promise of happiness be the truth of art, the truth about aesthetic experience, if this promise is something that we can no more understand than the riddle of art itself?" And later on: "Is art a *promise* of contentment at all, or is the experience of art not rather — at times — a *form* of contentment; a promise of contentment only in so far as every work of art promises us the contentment of an aesthetic experience?"[46]

---

46. Wellmer, "Das Versprechen des Glücks", (cf. 45), p. 20. Quotation within the quotation: Adorno, *Ästhetische Theorie* (cf. 12), p. 197.

I agree entirely with Wellmer on one point: it remains an anti-phenomenological act of violence to say about music that it is the apparential[47] invocation or anticipation of something whose historical or divine realisation has yet to come. To engage with its presence in the moment massively collides with the pre-condition of a non-apparential aspect *of* its apparency, which at the same time is only supposed to achieve self-realisation at some point in the distant future. *Adorno's negative theology is a way out, indeed an escape from the finitude of art and of aesthetic experience.* In Adorno's interpretation, what Heidegger refers to as the "quarrel between world and earth", the self-concealment in appearance and the self-revelation in self-withdrawal, the asemantic converse of meaning, the "riddle character" of art, its entire irresolvable ambiguity, congeals into the image of something *forthcoming*, i.e. a "promise", which can only be fulfilled in a possible, albeit a provisionally remote future, and which can only stake a claim to being more than a fleeting, ephemeral moment in relation to this forthcoming consummation. The fact that art's critical confrontation of society can only be justified through such a contingency of art on the mode of reality, and that only this can enable it to deny the status quo its demand of a reality to its "promise", i.e. to call to mind utopia without "betraying it to existence",[48] does not in itself guarantee the validity of the construction as such. Naturally Adorno is not a straightforward purveyor of the aesthetics of apparency; the category of the possible he is concerned with is not *simply*, but rather *even* possible. But because its utopian quality is as much ignited as it is consumed in the moment, it ultimately remains something provisional, something (albeit in the "higher" sense) as yet unfulfilled, which would for its part need to maintain its duration, constancy, steadfastness, and "reality" in relation to the continuing "omnipresence" of society's falsity in order to be inapparentially true, and to be referred to as such.

To restrict the moment of music to a mediatory significance

---

47. Translator's note: in keeping with the use of *apparency* for the German *Schein* elsewhere, this term has been coined to correspond to *scheinhaft*, which seems to have no more satisfactory equivalent in English.
48. Adorno, *Ästhetische Theorie* (cf. 12), p. 200.

whose realisation in time "has not yet begun",[49] only allowing us to sense the "potential" of itself "as if it had already become actual",[50] by necessity implies a bypassing of the musical event's presence and a subordination of its temporality to a truth that must remain transcendent. The moment is then no longer a moment: it is frozen in the horizon of a time that points to past and future *possibilities*, but remains external to the aesthetic activity itself. Music as an event is thus de-realised, even if such a de-realisation is not intended as a devaluation, but in fact as a celebration: "Only in the light of absolute, incorrodable individuation can there be any hope that precisely this has already existed and shall exist in the future; only through tending to this can the notion of the notion be fulfilled."[51]

There is a further aspect to this. As long as the continuing duration of the real in the shape of the not-yet-real is taken as the measure of the possible, the priority of the possible over the real is abstractly negated to the same degree as its ontological counter-force: the definitive non-being of possibility, the excessive impossibility of the real — death. One is even tempted to say: whoever does not want to speak of death should equally say nothing of utopia. Conclusional figures from reconciliatory philosophy only come about in the first place by not genuinely exposing themselves to a possible rupture through this "hardest of all counter-utopias" (Bloch), but rather springing directly from the antinomy implicit

---

49. Adorno, *Negative Dialektik* (*Gesammelte Schriften* vol.6), Frankfurt a. M. 1997, p. 148.
50. Adorno, *Ästhetische Theorie* (cf. 12), p. 364 (my italics, R.K.).
51. Adorno, *Negative Dialektik* (cf. 49), p. 366. In this structure lie at one and the same time the bases of both the truth and the apparency of art: truth, because, as an expression of the "omnipresence of the equivalential relation", it dissects that relation's substance through the medium of memory, thus reclaiming "the possible, as opposed to the real which ousted it" (*Ästhetische Theorie* [cf. 12], p. 204); apparency, because for its own phenomenal temporality, fulfilment and duration must by necessity remain transcendent, indeed because it "thus squanders the opportunity to create the possible which it produces as apparency." (op. cit., p. 129.) The fact that Adorno on other occasions speaks of the "moment" and the "explosion" as emphatically as after him only Karl Heinz Bohrer is not compatible with reconciliatory finalism (in either its good or bad forms). Cf. my contribution "Historie — Progreß — Augenblicklichkeit. Zur Hermeneutik musikalischer Erfahrung in der Moderne", in: Günther Pöltner (ed.), *Phänomenologie der Kunst*, Frankfurt a. M. 2000.

in the finite consciousness of the same.[52] Because negative dialectics only half-heartedly undertakes a critique of the suppression of death on the part of reconciliatory utopia, it continues the traditional allocation of transience and unfulfilment to the oneside, and constancy and fulfilment to the other, despite at the same time — or so it claims — being profoundly struck by sympathy for all that is alive and ephemeral. In speaking here of a tendency to envisage aesthetic experience without the "traits of finitude, of transience, of non-presence", he touches on a central point.

I also agree with Wellmer where he opposes Adorno's attempt to *identify* the immanent negativity of music not simply *as*, but ultimately *with* social criticism. Reconciliation as a — however impaired — constitutional reason of formal aesthetics, as the negatively theological vanishing point both of phenomenal analyses and of the ambitious undertaking to develop and focus the material and formal categories of specific works, is an untenable concept. If Adorno's writings on music show us anything, it is that distinctions such as those between "affirmation" and "radical critique", ideological enshroudment and enlightenment through negativity can only serve as criteria of an "engrossment in details" of compositional structures to a limited extent. This does not annul the validity of its demand that art should, for the sake of its own authenticity, absorb the negativity of the world into its own fabric and express it. But it does make one slightly sceptical of the thought-model through which Adorno sought to unfold and assert this demand.[53]

---

52. Cf. my contribution "Antinomien der Sterblichkeit. Reflexionen zu Heidegger und Adorno", in: *Internationale Zeitschrift für Philosophie* 1999/H. 1, pp. 140–174.

53. "This is only music; how must a world be composed in its entirety where questions of counterpoint alone testify to irreconcilable conflicts. (...) The shocks of the incomprehensible effected by artistic technique in the age of its own meaninglessness transform. They illuminate the senseless world. It is for this that new music sacrifices itself: it has taken all the darkness and guilt of the world upon itself. All its fortune lies in the recognition of misfortune; all its beauty lies in denying itself to the apparency of the beautiful. None want to have anything to do with it, whether individually or collectively. (...) It is the true message in a bottle." (Adorno, *Philosophie der neuen Musik* [cf. 25], pp. 11 & 126.) If there is a layer to Adorno's thought that strikes us as "historical", and nothing more, then surely this one. It should immediately be added: this does *not* obviate the necessity of a social interpretation of music as such, with all the tension between internal and external critique it involves.

My problems with Wellmer begin where he questions not only the historico-philosophical, but also the existential right of the place of utopia in aesthetic experience, and where, in his writing, time and timelessness, finitude and reconciliation, form and content collide dualistically like two independently existing worlds. One can probably agree quite readily on the fact that we are here situated on the edge of the conceivable; but even then, one must remember that this edge cannot have only one side.

Wellmer shares the anti-dialectical position occupied by Heidegger in *Sein und Zeit*.[54] I have already dealt with its virtues; its immediate problem, in my view, lies in its tendency to view the "timeless"—inasmuch as it cannot pacify it within an aesthetic context—as hocus-pocus, second-rate mysticism, as cognitively inaccessible and inexpressible, and therefore as philosophically irrelevant. Aside from the fact that the idea of Nirvana has a long and rich tradition, which can hardly be lost to art for the simple reason that it does not submit to the dualism of this life and the hereafter, of immanence and transcendence, one should inquire as to whether the plausible intention of mediating the moment of transcendence through the consciousness of finitude does not become a restrictive one if an entire field of experience is to be excluded from philosophical aesthetics simply because it cannot be adequately presented through the medium of theoretical argumentation. But the conflicts inherent in the passage cited above also result from Wellmer's implication that the issue at stake is that of forcing two utterly different spheres together, that there can be nothing timeless within time, that such an assumption is absurd *per se*. In supposing this, he for the most part equates timelessness with the figure shaped by Adorno's philosophy of reconciliation; he demonstrates its weakness, as I have already shown, with perfect accuracy. But is his aim equally sure outside the domain of historico-philosophical finalism? Wellmer ostensibly envisages the "otherness of time" as something which can by definition not be experienced by humans, i.e. as a realm of the beyond which erases

---

54. I am thinking here particularly of the passages on "eternity" and "immortality" in *Sein und Zeit* (cf. 20), p. 229 and 247 f.

the "traits of finitude, of transience, of non-presence" *a priori*. Because his critique only becomes more concrete in relation to the abstract antithetics of a leftist Hegelian philosophy of history, without even attempting to address a dialectic of the boundary, it secretly remains more dependent on a mere criticising than it seems to assume. In contrast to Hegel himself, his leftist disciples can no longer integrate historical progression into the present. Their "progressive" thought is always preconceived as crumbling apart into a discourse on the "radically historical", which polemicises against everything "eternal", and a utopian presence that congeals, after the "missed moment", to a mere remainder, to the "beyond" of all times. This actually rather curious renewal of the old dualist doctrine leads to the untenability of Adorno's reconciliatory concept, although he himself would certainly not have intended this. But does it follow from such a disregarding of presence that now "everything is history", and that we can, or even must dispense with transcendence? It honours the philosopher that he does not — unlike the theologian — desire the "leap". But is a temporal and finitudal monism an adequate response to the collapse of grand metaphysical utopias, including socialism? I can accept a clear preference for the autonomy of the work in the face of global futurological constructions of any kind; I simply fail to understand why this should be exaggerated so defensively that art is ultimately cut off from the possibility of developing an impulse that transcends existence.

Theunissen ultimately proves right inasmuch as he unreservedly takes the dialectic of the boundary seriously: we misconceive the otherness of time in envisaging it as the beyond, and — Platonically — setting it in opposition to the ephemeral world of the senses as the realm of the eternal. What is important is rather the fact that "even if we must not allow it to *solidify into the different*, we must still *hold onto it as that which differs.*"[55] Temporality may be irrevocable for us, but this does not make finitude absolute. Not only can our life not be "envisaged without" the

---

55. Theunissen, "Die Einheit im Denken Georg Pichts", in: *Merkur* 37 (1983), pp. 780–790, here p. 789.

yearning for a freedom from time; we also experience this freedom — as always — in an "impaired" form. We experience it, for example, in the knowledge of our death, which anticipates this exit from the here and now of time. And even if we ourselves cannot know exactly what it actually is that we know, even if we are always also concealing something inconceivable, we should still "hold onto" the fact that this concealment of knowledge not only discharges us into the tautness of the temporal dimensions, into the game of the world, but also distances us — in the midst of this game, in the midst of time — from time as such, i.e. from our lives as a whole. Art is an excellent tool for rendering this "nullity of thought" accessible to our experience, for giving it a place in which to discover the hereness of its otherness. Art is a confrontation with the boundaries of our finite existence, it develops relationships to these, it rebels against them and goes beyond them: virtuosic, performative, unserious, contemplative, inconspicuous, ideological, complex. It is not, as Picht claims, simply the human answer to the certainty of death, but also an expression of man's creative ignorance of the end, of playing with the inconceivable, at the same time the voice of seriousness and metaphysical spleen. *Perhaps it is only through the demise of the reconciliatory idea, both as a historico-philosophical model and as the normative concept of a "higher critique", that we can at all define the content of its existential experience more closely, and thus release the idea of a freedom from time from the odium of the mere leap of faith.*

If "love and death" are among the "great themes of art", as Wellmer emphasises,[56] then this presumably relates not so much to Romeo and Juliet as to the material, the form, the language and the structure of works — and their phenomenal presentation in the moment. It does not hold water to accord the artistic "concern" for the end of our existence a certain relevance to our worldly life at the level of "grand themes", i.e. of subjects and material, while presenting these matters as secondary or even meaningless at the formal level simply because the historico-

---

56. Wellmer, "Das Versprechen des Glücks" (cf. 45), p. 28.

philosophical aesthetics of apparency has proved as untenable as it always has been. Wellmer could say in response to this that it is not his concern to dismiss existential threshold problems as secondary; that he simply believes that, in art, even "last questions" are present only as aesthetically reflected and reflecting ones, and that the question of what this means cannot be elucidated through recourse to the "last questions" themselves. In any case, he might continue, art is — on account of the fundamental ambiguity of its formal language — not only constitutionally unsuited to pacifying the metaphysical needs of our senses, but in fact almost *the* primary counterforce to the "terror of a ... final and comprehensive sense."[57] Unquestionably, it is perfectly sensible to posit the aesthetic domain as a discourse of subversion against the appropriation of art through totalist political and ideological agendas. It also reminds us of the necessity of not confusing aesthetic phenomena with religious ones, but rather also describing and analysing them with aesthetic methods. But nonetheless: art alone cannot explain art. The consistency with which Wellmer defends its autonomy

---

57. Wellmer, "Adorno, die Moderne und das Erhabene" (cf. 45), p. 203. The *political* and *ethical* motive of Wellmer's critique of reconciliatory philosophy in aesthetic matters, and his understanding of autonomy and finitude, gains an exemplary clarity in certain statements which, in terms of their subject matter, belong to his critique of Adorno, but in their context are directed against the early Marx. They deal with the utopian promises of fulfilled time, mystical transfiguration and revolutionary action: "But it would be an error of thought to take those promises literally, i.e. politically: it would amount to a secret aestheticisation of the political — not in the fascist sense, but in the manner of the early Romantics. Works of art and moments of fulfilled time might be perfect; historical reality will never be, as the annulment of its negativity would constitute an annulment of its temporality. (...) If one... examines history in terms of a sense that can be perfected, in terms of a possible perfection of the forms of human life, then one can no longer do justice to those aspects of it that are imperfect; and ultimately not to the genuine human beings in their uniqueness, their otherness and their rights. This is the inhumanity of Marx's humanism, or rather: the potential of his inhumanity." (Wellmer, "Bedeutet das Ende des "realen Sozialismus" auch das Ende des Marxschen Humanismus? Zwölf Thesen", in: *Endspiele: Die unversöhnliche Moderne* [cf. 45], p. 93). Cf. *Metaphysik im Augenblick ihres Sturzes*, op. cit., p. 212 on the "incurable conflict between materialist and metaphysical (i.e. theological) motives" in Adorno's aesthetics. For Wellmer, the notions of justice and truth definitely transcend the realm of the finite; art, however, does not.

sometimes — in spite of all tendencies to the contrary[58] — risks diminishing its world-relations, or even reducing them to a mere remainder or external factor: if ultimately nothing remained of the contentment which — according to Stendhal and Adorno — aesthetic experience promises us but the contentment of the aesthetic experience itself, i.e. if the utopia were made to retreat into the empirical experience of the blessed apparency, then it could presumably no longer even be made plausible why "love and death" supposedly constitute two of the "grand themes of art".

VI.

A fundamental aspect of the musical event's substance is the fact that within it, one finds oneself — in a certain sense — simultaneously inside and outside the horizon of one's own life-span. The shock of the "only this once and never agin" experience, suddenness, irreversibility *and* fulfilled presence: these vital elements of musical experience would be incomprehensible if their existence served only successivity as such, i.e. in the mere sequence of the appearance, progression and vanishing of sounds, and not equally in that which enables us to experience the radical transience of this medium as a whole in the first place. Neither can the temporality of music be deduced from the present mode of our existence and its temporal dimensionalisation. Both the successivity of global time and the modal network of mortal time are, of course, integral conditions for the musical event. They do not explain, however — or at least not adequately —, the event itself, its concentration, as it were, of a whole life within a moment and the specific liaison between ecstasy and distance that dominates any experience of it.

One says of certain moments that they are "eternal", not in spite of, but rather because of their unrepeatability. What one means is that the intensity of the event which makes such a moment what

---

58. Cf. in particular "Das Versprechen des Glücks" (cf. 45), p. 32: "Art must render the weight of the world palpable, visible and audible if its subsumption of the world into its game is to have aesthetic weight."

it is cannot be grasped in terms of the conditions of temporal succession. It rather bursts into these as if from without, and the newness thus released is such that one can say: it throws me off my course *and*, at the same time, guides me towards a reflexive distance from it, i.e. from the continuum of my previous self-understanding. The moment belongs neither to the scheme of time nor to a timeless presence beyond it. Its "eternity" lies in its elemental discontinuity and in an expulsion from the conventional contexts of life; one cannot assume any durational demands on its part, any more than one can think of it as an ephemeral *now* and nothing more.

In relation to the instantaneity of music, this definition proves insufficient. Obviously the musical moment cannot be deduced from the perspective of before and after, as it takes place so to speak in the space between time and timelessness. The basic feature of a sudden expulsion from the continuum of the ordinary, however, characterises a number of experiential forms, but does not tell us anything specific about the structure of musical time. This specificity only becomes visible if one interprets the temporal structure of music itself with the context of our life-span, i.e. also: *if one reveals the otherness of time in the musical phenomenon to the same degree that one then connects its transcendence to the horizon of finite listening.*

The notion of the musical moment as the abbreviation of life from the cradle to the grave is more than the somewhat eccentric metaphor it initially appears to be. For it does not simply name the joyous fulfilment of what Picht calls the "singularity of the hour"[59] — it also reveals precisely what consitutes this fulfilment, namely assuming a position outside time, inhabiting a particular time-span while living beyond life. The experience of music reveals a perspective that must by necessity remain undiscovered as long as we occupy "the standpoint of finitude"[60] absolutely, i.e. as long as we understand the irrevocable temporal dimensionality of our existence as or like being "buried alive in the earth". It is here not a matter of leaping out of finitude, be it in a Platonic or Christian

---

59. Picht, *Grundlinien einer Philosophie der Musik* (cf. 2), p. 425.
60. Gadamer, *Wahrheit und Methode* (cf. 33), p. 105.

manner or otherwise. It is rather a matter of, as it were, dicovering locations, points, tips at which the relation to its boundaries becomes apparent, or to be more precise: where the possibility to establish a relationship to finitude in general, and thus to its — and one's own — boundaries offers or opens itself. All transcendence remains tied to the structural conditions of our existence, and to a certain extent "simply" shapes these individually; Heidegger insisted on this in his early work, and rightly so. But this tie does not already condemn it to a mere apparency, to a tranquilliser which simply suppresses the "being unto death" and other fatalities; nor is it a reason to fix one's view on one side of the boundary and avoid any dialectical relationship between the two like the plague.

We know that our life has a beginning and an end, that we are born and will die. But these "outer extremes" of existence elude our experience, as they precede it, even condition it. We know of the beginning and end, but know nothing *about* them. Listening to music is like moving beyond this blind spot while remaining within it. A musical work does not simply have a beginning and an end, it rather connects these in a meaningful way; precisely this is beyond human capacity. Humans can create works which connect their beginning and their end, but cannot turn their life into such a work.[61] On the one hand, musical listening — and musical performance all the more — is a radical experience of mortality: the unrepeatability of a particular performance can be so overwhelming that the mere fact of, for example, a suitcase full of Bach's organ works — a symbol of that which is structurally repeatable about them — seems no longer comprehensible, almost like a messenger from another world. But the liaison between ecstasy and distance mentioned above encompasses the imposition of an abstraction: we could not actually have this radical experience of mortality if we were not also able to experience it as if completely from the outside and relate it to a horizon that rises beyond it. The intensity of the musical moment consists in the fact that

---

61. Gadamer enjoys citing the following statement by Alcmaion of Croton: "Humans must die on account of their inability to connect their end back to their beginning." (*Die Zeitanschauung des Abendlandes*, in: Gadamer, *Neuere Philosophie II* [*Gesammelte Werke* vol. 4], Tübingen 1999, p. 123)

this moment is not consumed in the immediacy of its consummation, but rather always thematicises it, as it were examines it, as an ethnologist might examine his own native culture. Listening to music means experiencing transience in a state of intoxication, yet also being slightly absent from it, perceiving one's own temporal life as if faced with an "eternal" counterpart or contrast.

One could raise the following objection: that I am guilty of confusing aesthetic and metaphysical expectations and thus sacrificing music's autonomous sense of purpose to a spirit world in the blink of an eye; and that, in addition, my critique of Adorno's reconciliatory thinking and my partially positive reference to Heidegger's ontology of finitude contradict this. This charge, however, presumes a system to these deliberations which they do not have. I have so far said nothing of reconciliation, nor do I consider myself to have arrived in the no man's land between theology and materialism in which Adorno is at home. Nor am I concerned with final justifications or even salvations. *I am simply attempting to give a traditionally metaphysical notion an — in the widest possible sense — existential or anthropological turn, and to determine the experiential context it circles around and which — as a form of metaphysics, i.e. because of an "eschatological" expectation or interest — it nonetheless evades.* In doing so, however, I avoid simply attributing the paradoxical structure of temporal experience in music to the apparency that blissfully appears in itself. Nor can the necessity of a phenomenology of specifically compositional structures in itself constitute an argument for removing the rift between metaphysics and existence from aesthetics altogether like an irksome foreign body. For it is precisely this rift that I am interested in.

Perhaps Adorno would still essentially have sympathised with this. But the entire debate would probably have struck him as "too subjectivistic", as an offloading of a fundamental speculative problem onto the contingency of individual experience. His work-idea ultimately remains, in spite of all its dialectics, too strongly indebted to the model of the final object for him to have seen in the incorporation of the temporality of the listener's and the performer's own lives in the autonomous temporal structure of music, in the constellative combination of composed time and immediate linear time, anything other than an apologist concession to the empirical, a dilution of the monad in favour of contexts of social effect. I, however, am concerned neither with descriptive psychology nor with market research, but rather — specifically — with ontology. My topic is not primarily the listener's or performer's experience as such, but rather the structures — set and represented (not alone) by the work — in which this experience occurs, regardless of whether it refers to them consciously or not. The point of departure, however, remains the constellation comprising the moment and the composed form, the temporality of the work and of the listener's life. I do not address "threshold problems" for the sake of an ultimate metaphysical justification or a finality of fulfilment, but rather with reference to their finitude and relevance to life, which amounts to the following: the barrier at the frontline between artistic experience and world-experience has always been dismantled already.

Adorno, on the other hand, sets up a sudden and direct collision between a substantialist notion of the work and a positivist notion of its reception, inasmuch as it is not entirely subsumed by an adequate understanding of the work.[62] The work is envisaged and recognised as autonomous to the extent that it withdraws, even shuts itself off negationally from all concrete experiential contexts. The dimension of an "external" experience or interpretration of it is only meaningful in so far as it can be attributed to the "inner" instructions and "demands" of the "matter itself"; everything beyond this is lost in the ideology of the factual. Consequently, the dialectic of time and timelessness is reduced to a process that takes place "objectively" in the work or which the work carries out "within itself". Forms of medial representation are not even mentioned in this, let alone problematised.

Adorno's normative, one might even say dogmatic preference for

---

62. "Problems of reception and communication can only arise in the context of art if the referential connection between reality, the work and utopia is questioned. Where this referential context is assumed, on the other hand, problems of reception and communication exhaust themselves in the problem of an appropriate way to grasp the referential context itself." (Albrecht Wellmer, "Wahrheit, Schein, Versöhnung. Adornos ästhetische Rettung der Modernität", in: *Zur Dialektik von Moderne und Postmoderne. Vernunftkritik nach Adorno*, Frankfurt a. M. 1985, p. 23 f.)

Beethoven's intensive temporality at least becomes comprehensible, in a certain sense even consistent through this. It transpires as the result of a union between a radical philosophical notion of artistic autonomy and certain means and possibilities of formal shaping in music; these latter establish a new paradigm of temporality and historicity which achieves an integration of extremes unprecedented in all previous music: in Beethoven's music, one could say, the monad trembles in revolutionary manner within itself *and* maintains its distance to the theatre of the world; the eternal present displays history as a storm *and* opposes its abandonment to transience; the open future and the meaningful whole mediate amongst themselves *and* retain their connection to a centre which they do not abandon. Beethoven's temporally intensive works are, for Adorno, the measure of all music, for they are more than single compositions — it is through them that a horizon of musical thought is accessed in the first place. Certainly the ahistorical tendency of this model is not acceptable: simply because the speculative philosophical notion has here found, as it were, its musico-historical place, there is no higher necessity to extrapolate the "ideal of all music" from this. One can very well understand, however, the reason for Adorno's normative orientation according to this historical moment and no other. Not only is the self-critical aspect — which subsequently establishes a referential context with regard to "extensive" corrections and alternatives — latent in the intensive form of temporality; autonomy is in fact understood in such a complex sense here that it allows us to recognise the experiential dimension which I have above termed — with reference to the musical event — a rift between existential and metaphysical temporal experience as a conflict which is undergone and expressed in the inner core of the works themselves: "moments of transcendence"[63] is Adorno's term for precisely those passages in Beethoven where a pointedly innovative musical figure or figuration bursts in on the entire processual context of immanence — as

---

63. Adorno, *Beethoven* (cf. 11), p. 37. Cf. also his statements on the "moment" and "breakthrough" in Mahler's music, in: *Mahler. Eine musikalische Physiognomik*, in: *Die musikalischen Monographien* (*Gesammelte Schriften* vol. 13), Frankfurt a. M. 1997, chap. 1, esp. p. 152 ff.

it were like a "paranormal" event — from without. (In contrast to Adorno, I am thinking less of the D flat major passage in the Adagio of the first *Rasumovsky* quartet or the F major theme in the slow movement of the piano sonata op. 31/2 than the oboe recitative in the recapitulation of the first movement of the Fifth Symphony — a "moment of transcendence" in the perhaps most "intensive" piece of music that Beethoven wrote: an intrusion from without on a process of immanent transgression.)

One could even go a step further, and say: the tension between existence and metaphysics, between a dimensionalised life-span and the speculative negation of time, attains representation in precisely the relationship connecting intensive and extensive temporal forms. It is no coincidence that Adorno's analyses of the *Archduke* trio and the *Pastorale* are among the very few parts of his writings which at all thematicise experience in relation to the temporal dimensionalisation of immediacy.[64]

Beethoven's music is, after all, a rich proof of the fact that metaphysical ideas of utopia, reconciliation, freedom from time etc. were not simply added from without by an imperial philosophers' rationale of art, but for a considerable part stem from its own formal and expressive organisation. In the works of the "middle" period, at any rate, there is a dominance of something like a balance between autonomy and utopia: the utopian substance has not yet withdrawn into the negativity of critical materialist reflection, and still radiates from the whole of the immanent form, and as an immanent whole. Utopia is realised either as a negation of an internally negative process which posits every moment as unfulfilled and exceeds it: transcendence through transgression.

---

64. It is clear why this is not the case in the passages on the intensive symphonies and sonatas: the time which one is exposed to, which penetrates the listener, can only be positively experienced once the demand for its breathless subsumption in the spirit, as it were, is no longer unreservedly valid, and has rather made way for a comparatively assured mimetic passivity. Only when time is no longer "experienced as a hostile resistance that destroys the illusion of an unlimited continuance through its ability to command time" (Gadamer, "Über leere und erfüllte Zeit", in: *Neuere Philosophie II* [cf. 62], p. 141), can it reveal itself as that leeway in life which can contentedly be dwelt in.

Or, on the other hand, it is the counterpart to the totality, and suspends it externally and specifically in the moment: transcendence through irruption.[65] The works can, as it were, not rest easy with their autonomy, but rather strive beyond it; but they cannot leave it behind or beneath them, as this would betray the claim to freedom which they themselves articulate. The reference to an "other state" is a necessary part of the intensive temporal form's construction *and* that of its extensive deviations, and was such long before Bloch and Adorno sought to impose it.

The emphatic ideality of this position, as I have already argued, is no longer present, and can no longer be made present. One must not, however, repeat Adorno's mistake in reverse by responding to his positing of a particular historical situation as an absolute with a total historicisation and culturalisation of the utopian. One should rather be able to say what is valid about an argument which wrongly sought to reclaim the "image of the end of transience" as the "ideal of music" with reference to Beethoven's intensive temporality in the first place.

Perhaps we are only dealing with this one initially quite simple insight: time is not everything (even) in music. Music rather rebels against it in the name of a present which gathers and concentrates its dimensions within itself. This rebellion is successful inasmuch as its presence exists in and of itself, i.e. cannot be deduced from the scheme of before and after. At the same time, it fails, as it remains dominated by the very transience it opposes. The musical work, however, combines the two and represents them: it turns, as it were, this ambivalence of time and timelessness, transience and presence into something positive by enduring the strain between its various aspects. It has this capacity in so far as it is not entirely at the mercy of the power of transience, and can instead maintain its distance from it and act in relation to it, even in representation of it. The work is able to render time present in all its inhomogeneity for the very reason that it does not entirely belong to it.

Nonetheless, this is only one side of the matter, and is inaccessible without the other: the temporal deconstruction of the work-

---

65. The distinction between these two forms of transcendence (transgression / irruption) stems from lectures held by Theunissen.

idea, the temporalisation of its internal relations with reference to representational media, the event, the game and reception. In this manner—to put it conservatively—, substance is changed into contingency, absolute truth is exposed to a dynamic of pluralisation, and first—or last—questions of the spirit are made finite in the context of existential threshold experiences. Without a withdrawal of fundamentalist justificatory expectations, however, there could be no meaningful talk of speculative experiential content in aesthetics whatsoever.

After all, the history of musical modernism—as Adorno has shown—is not least the history of a compositional destruction of the "intensive" notion of time revolving around successivity, development and "introduction", and its transformation into forms of "statistical" or "spatialised" temporality.[66] Yet this has nothing to do with a simple alternative in the sense of spatialisation or development, extensity or intensity, modalised temporality or successive linearity. Such a clear opposition between diverging temporal forms has rather been replaced by a multiplicity of different, indeed heterogeneous forms which can no longer be assigned to one type or identifiable mode of mediation or another. Stasis and plurality, spatialisation and non-identity, indifference and diversity belong together as characteristic compositional tendencies in the 20th century; they are two—ambivalent—sides of the same coin, namely the loss of any unifying integral in music. To use Adorno's terminology: the intensive temporal type no longer provides the normative horizon of unity with reference to

---

66. As great as the differences between "schools" may be, there is at least agreement between them that they, compared to Beethoven, realise without exception a "static", stationary, a-developmental experience of time. Music increasingly seems a "becoming" within which—in spite of all rapid movements, high speeds and racing turbulences at the local level—on the whole "nothing happens", i.e. whose sound-events can no longer be forced together in the sense of a process which unfolds, so to speak, through its own force; the material simply no longer allows it. Serial composers, for example, see themselves confronted with the question of "how time" can "pass" in a non-trivial sense if neither its harmonic totality nor its rhythmic-metric syntax (pre)-structures the continuum of events any longer. Their question is: can one still move at all "convincingly" from one moment to the next, or is successivity to be abandoned as a means of orientation in favour of creating an adjacency of separate sound-points or composing with "groups", or in favour of a new understanding of "space"?

which all other temporal concepts can subsequently be determined and evaluated. It is itself diminished, so to speak, to a specific perspective of temporal experience, it can — though certainly still binding *as* a perspective — no longer claim to be central for the constitution of criteria (assuming it ever could make this claim). The possibility of interpreting the many forms of temporal experience in music in terms of a final, universal point of identity has vanished, i.e. become historical. But: everything depends on not one-sidedly interpreting this situation as a loss, or as a sinister overpowering of the subject through the "rule of time".

At the same time, it seems to me, a deciding element of truth remains in Adorno's construction. When he writes: "One can no longer compose as Beethoven did, but one must think as he composed",[67] one should not take this as a dogmatic apologia for the model of through-composed developmental history. It is rather a matter of the intention and the capacity of music to counter the flow of time by seeking to follow it and confront each of its boundaries. To put it differently: in place of the grand utopia of the "introduction of time as an image of the end of transience" we find the plain, yet insistent desire to resist time by following a "goal" that offers both a precarious freedom from its successional constitution and, simultaneously, absorbs within itself the force of that from which it offers freedom. A single moment is at stake here, an impulse, a tendency against the "universalisation and affirmation" of time, not the process as an emphatic totality or "progress". Without this impulse against time, against successivity, against its own passing, music would not be music. The temporal art *par excellence* thrives on its confrontation of the very thing which it makes its art. In any case, it is not the antinomy between time and non-time, presence and transience, finitude and infinity that has disappeared, but rather the possibility of establishing a stable balance between these opposites.

---

67. Adorno, *Beethoven* (cf. 11), p. 231.

PERSONALIA

JONATHAN CROSS

Jonathan Cross taught at the Universities of Sussex (1986–95) and Bristol (1996–2003) before joining the Oxford Music Faculty in 2003. He has written, lectured and broadcast widely on issues in contemporary music and he has made a particular study of the work of Harrison Birtwistle, including the book *Harrison Birtwistle: Man, Mind, Music* (Faber/Cornell University Press, 2000).

His highly-acclaimed book *The Stravinsky Legacy* was published in 1998 by CUP. He is also editor of *Music Analysis* (Blackwell Publishers). Recent and forthcoming publications include articles on Schoenberg and Stravinsky, Finnissy and Ferneyhough, essays on Birtwistle for two CUP volumes (on traditions of music theory and analysis in Europe in the twentieth century), a study of 20th-century British music and institutions for the Einaudi *Enciclopedia della Musica* and contributions to the revised *New Grove* and *Musik in Geschichte und Gegenwart*.

Professor Cross is editor of and contributor to the *Cambridge Companion to Stravinsky* (CUP, 2003). In April 2002, he directed the 5th European Music Analysis Conference, held at the Bristol Music Department.

JONATHAN HARVEY

Jonathan Harvey was a chorister at St Michael's College, Tenbury and later a major music scholar at St John's College, Cambridge. He gained doctorates from the universities of Glasgow and Cambridge and also studied privately (on the advice of Benjamin Britten) with Erwin Stein and Hans Keller. He was a Harkness Fellow at Princeton (1969–70).

An invitation from Boulez to work at IRCAM in the early 1980s has resulted in eight realisations at the Institute, or for the Ensemble Intercontemporain, including the tape piece *Mortuos Plango Vivos Voco*, *Ritual Melodies* for computer-manipulated sounds, and *Advaya* for cello and live and pre-recorded sounds. Harvey has also composed in most other genres: orchestra (including *White as Jasmine*), chamber (including *Soleil Noir* and *Chitra*), choir (*Mothers shall not Cry*), opera (*Passion and Resurrection*) as well as works for solo instruments.

Harvey now attracts commissions from many international organisations. His music has been extensively played and toured by, amongst others, Ensemble Modern, Ensemble InterContemporain, and Ictus Ensemble of Brussels. He is regularly performed at all the major international contemporary music festivals, and is one of the most skilled and imaginative composers working in electronic music. He has honorary doctorates from the universities of Southampton and Bristol, is a Member of Academia Europaea, and in 1993 was awarded the prestigious Britten Award for composition. He published two books in 1999, on inspiration and spirituality respectively. He was Visiting Professor of Music at Imperial College, London and is Honorary Professor at Sussex University.

HELMUT LACHENMANN

Helmut Lachenmann studied piano with Jürgen Uhde and composition and theory with Johann Nepomuk David at the Stuttgart Musikhochschule. He was also the first student of Luigi Nono in Venice. In 1965 he worked at the electronic music studio at the University of Ghent.

Lachenmann received numerous awards, including the Kulturpreis für Musik from the city of Munich (1965), the Bach-Preis Hamburg (1972) and a honorary doctorate from the Hannover Musikhochschule (2001). He is a member of the Akademie der Künste in Berlin, Hamburg, Leipzig, Mannheim and Munich and the Academie voor Wetenschappen, Letteren en Schone Kunsten van België.

Professor Lachenmann taught at the Stuttgart Musikhochschule from 1966–70, the Pädagogische Hochschule in Ludwigsburg from 1970–76, the University of Basle in 1972–73 and the Hannover Musikhochschule from 1976–81. Since 1978, he has been an instructor at Darmstadt and since 1981, he has been Professor für Komposition at the Stuttgart Musikhochschule. In addition he has lectures all over the world.

His music has been featured at festivals throughout the world, including the Ars Musica (Brussels), the Darmstadt, the Festival d'Automne (Paris), the Tage für Neue Musik (Stuttgart), the Venice Biennale, the Wien Modern (Vienna) and the Tage für Neue Musik (Zürich). In 2002 the Salzburg Festival featured five portrait concerts of his work, as well as a symposium about his œuvre.

Personalia

ALBRECHT WELLMER

Albrecht Wellmer taught philosophy in Frankfurt, Toronto, New York, and Konstanz. He has been a philosophy professor at Freie Universität Berlin since 1990 (emeritus since 2001). In addition to countless papers on practical philosophy, critical theory, aesthetics and language philosophy, he has published, amongst others, *Zur Dialektik von Moderne und Postmoderne. Vernunftkritik nach Adorno* (Frankfurt a.M. 1985); *Ethik und Dialog. Elemente des moralischen Urteils bei Kant und in der Diskursethik* (Frankfurt a.M. 1986); *Endspiele: Die unversöhnliche Moderne. Essays und Vorträge* (Frankfurt a.M. 1993); *Revolution und Interpretation* (Amsterdam 1998).

RICHARD KLEIN

Richard Klein studied organ, church music and music education, took an A degree for concerts and recorded for radio stations. He then went on to study musicology, philosophy, theology and modern literature. His Ph.D. thesis was about Adorno's criticism of Wagner. As professor, he teaches organ and music theory, lectures philosophy and is regularly invited as a guest lecturer by other national and international universities and colleges. He is also the scientific advisor of the Stuttgart Staatsoper and the editor of *Musik & Ästhetik*.

Publications (selection): *Mit den Ohren denken. Adornos Philosophie der Musik* (1998); *Antinomien der Sterblichkeit. Reflexionen zu Heidegger und Adorno* (1999); *Musik in der Zeit — Zeit in der Musik* (2000); *Narben des Gesamtkunstwerks. Wagners "Ring des Nibelungen"* (2001); *Mit und gegen Adorno. Zur Präsenz seines Denkens* (co-editor, 2004). He is currently writing a book about Bob Dylan.

EDITORS
Frank Agsteribbe, Sylvester Beelaert,
Peter Dejans, Jeroen D'hoe

AUTHORS
Jonathan Cross
Jonathan Harvey
Helmut Lachenmann
Albrecht Wellmer
Richard Klein

TRANSLATION
Wieland Hoban
XLNt Communication

LAY-OUT
Filiep Tacq, Ghent

PRESS
Grafikon, Oostkamp
Bioset, 100gr

ISBN 90 5867 413 4
D/2004/1869/63
NUR 663
© 2004 by Leuven University Press /
Universitaire Pers Leuven / Presses Universitaires de Louvain
Blijde-Inkomststraat 5, B-3000 Leuven (Belgium)

All rights reserved.
Except in those cases expressly determined by law,
no part of this publication may be multiplied,
saved in automated data file or made public in any way whatsoever
without the express prior written consent of the publishers.

www.ingramcontent.com/pod-product-compliance
Lightning Source LLC
Chambersburg PA
CBHW050633160426
43194CB00010B/1660